3rd Edition

Ventures Basic

WORKBOOK

Gretchen Bitterlin ▪ **Dennis Johnson** ▪ **Donna Price** ▪ **Sylvia Ramirez**

K. Lynn Savage (Series Editor)

CAMBRIDGE
UNIVERSITY PRESS

CAMBRIDGE
UNIVERSITY PRESS

University Printing House, Cambridge CB2 8BS, United Kingdom

One Liberty Plaza, 20th Floor, New York, NY 10006, USA

477 Williamstown Road, Port Melbourne, VIC 3207, Australia

314–321, 3rd Floor, Plot 3, Splendor Forum, Jasola District Centre, New Delhi – 110025, India

79 Anson Road, #06–04/06, Singapore 079906

Cambridge University Press is part of the University of Cambridge.

It furthers the University's mission by disseminating knowledge in the pursuit of education, learning and research at the highest international levels of excellence.

www.cambridge.org
Information on this title: www.cambridge.org/9781108449984

© Cambridge University Press 2018

First published 2008
Second edition 2014

20 19 18 17 16 15 14 13 12 11 10 9 8 7 6 5 4 3 2

Printed in Mexico by Editorial Impresora Apolo, S.A. de C.V.

A catalogue record for this publication is available from the British Library

ISBN 978-1-108-44953-3 Student's Book
ISBN 978-1-108-44966-3 Literacy Workbook
ISBN 978-1-108-44932-8 Online Workbook
ISBN 978-1-108-57321-4 Teacher's Edition
ISBN 978-1-108-44919-9 Class Audio CDs
ISBN 978-1-108-45027-0 Presentation Plus

Additional resources for this publication at www.cambridge.org/ventures

CONTENTS

WELCOME

1 Write the letters.

A   B   C   D   E   F

G   ___   I   J   K   ___

M   N   O   ___   Q   R

S   ___   U   V   W   ___

Y   Z

2 Write the letters.

a   b   c   d   e   ___

g   h   ___   j   k   ___

m   n   ___   p   q   ___

s   t   ___   v   w   ___

y   z

3 **Listen and number.**

a. __1__

b. ____

c. ____

d. ____

e. ____

f. ____

g. ____

h. ____

i. ____

Check your answers. See page 131.
WELCOME **3**

4 Write the numbers.

1	2	3	___	5
6	___	8	9	___
11	12	___	14	15
___	17	18	___	20

5 Write the numbers.

one	two	___
four	___	six
___	eight	___
ten	eleven	___
thirteen	___	fifteen
___	seventeen	___
nineteen	___	

6 Look at the pictures. Write the numbers.

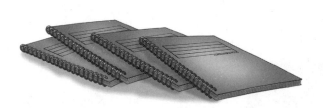

1. _____four_____

2. _____

3. _____

4. _____

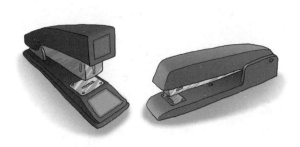

5. _____

6. _____

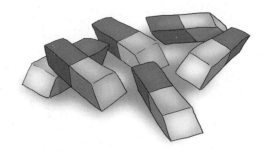

7. _____

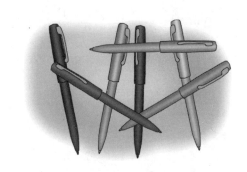

8. _____

Check your answers. See page 131. **WELCOME 5**

Lesson A Listening

1 **Look at the ID card. Write the words.**

STUDENT ID CARD

1 Anna   2 Lopez
first name   last name
3 Mexico
country
4 254   5 555-2992
area code   phone number

1. <u>f</u> <u>i</u> <u>r</u> <u>s</u> <u>t</u> <u>n</u> <u>a</u> <u>m</u> <u>e</u>

2. ___ ___ ___ ___ ___ ___ ___ ___

3. ___ ___ ___ ___ ___ ___

4. ___ ___ ___ ___ ___ ___ ___

5. ___ ___ ___ ___ ___ ___ ___ ___ ___ ___

2 **Write the words and numbers from Exercise 1.**

1. <u>A</u> <u>n</u> <u>n</u> <u>a</u>
   first name

2. ___ ___ ___ ___ ___
   last name

3. ___ ___ ___ ___ ___ ___
   country

4. ___ ___ ___
   area code

5. ___ ___ ___ - ___ ___ ___ ___
   phone number

3 Listen and write the number.

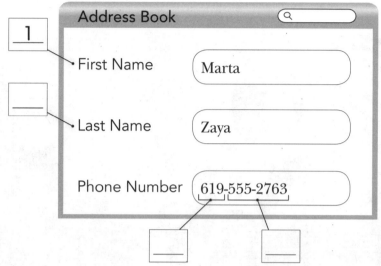

Address Book

| 1 | First Name | Marta |

| ___ | Last Name | Zaya |

Phone Number | 619-555-2763

___ ___

4 Write the words.

area code   first name   last name   phone number

1. (917) 555-4980 _____ phone number

2. (917) 555-4980 _____

3. John Smith _____

4. John Smith _____

5 Write the words.

area code   first name   last name   phone number

phonepages

J JOHNSON–JONES

1. _____ first name _____

Craig Johnson   (786) 555-0874

3. _____

Vera Johnson   (385) 555-1232

2. _____

4. _____

Lesson B Countries

1 **Look at the picture. Match. Write the letter.**

Diane Binh Lorena Kalifa Fabio Shen Yuri Flore

1. __f__ Binh   a. Brazil

2. ____ Fabio   b. China

3. ____ Kalifa   c. Mexico

4. ____ Lorena   d. Russia

5. ____ Shen   e. Somalia

6. ____ Yuri   f. Vietnam

7. ____ Diane   g. Haiti

8. ____ Flore   h. the United States

2 **Unscramble the letters. Write the countries.**

1. C n a h i _____   4. e x M i o c _____

2. z i l B a r _____   5. o m S l i a a _____

3. s s i a R u _____   6. i H i t a _____

3 **Look at the picture. Write the countries.**

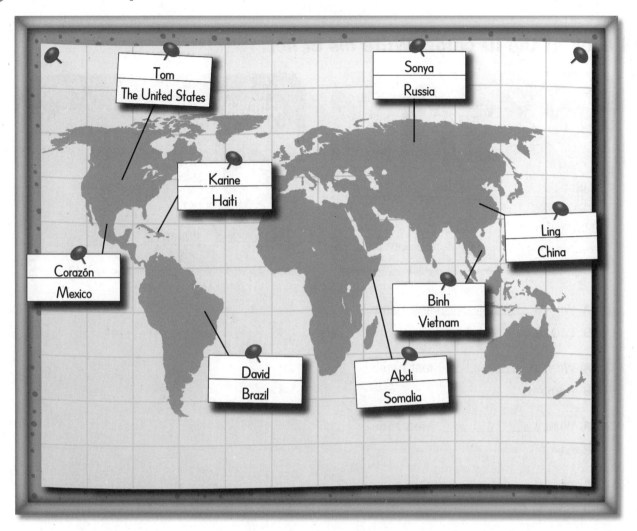

1. Where is Abdi from?   _____Somalia_____.

2. Where is Tom from?   _____.

3. Where is Ling from?   _____.

4. Where is David from?   _____.

5. Where is Sonya from?   _____.

6. Where is Corazón from?   _____.

7. Where is Karine from?   _____.

8. Where is Binh from?   _____.

Lesson C What's your name?

1 **Look at the ID cards. Write *his* or *her*.**

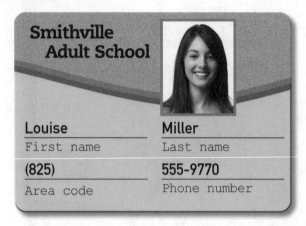

1. **A** What's _____her_____ first name?
   B Louise.

2. **A** What's _____ last name?
   B Ramirez.

3. **A** What's _____ area code?
   B 614.

4. **A** What's _____ phone number?
   B 555-9770.

5. **A** What's _____ area code?
   B 825.

6. **A** What's _____ first name?
   B Carlos.

7. **A** What's _____ last name?
   B Miller.

8. **A** What's _____ phone number?
   B 555-8052.

2 Write *My* or *your*.

Alan   What's _____your_____ first name?
                              1

Manuel   _____ first name is Manuel.
                        2

Alan   What's _____ last name?
                              3

Manuel   _____ last name is Alvez.
                        4

Alan   What's _____ area code?
                              5

Manuel   _____ area code is 917.
                        6

Alan   What's _____ phone number?
                              7

Manuel   _____ phone number is 555-9845.
                        8

3 Complete the form about Manuel.

Job Interview Notes

First name: _Manuel_____

Last name: _____

Area code: _____

Phone number: _____

Lesson D Reading

1 Circle the answers.

Hello

First name	*Boris*
Last name	*Egorov*
Country	*Russia*

1. His name is _____ . (Boris Egorov)   Egorov Boris

2. His last name is _____ .   Boris   Egorov

3. His first name is _____ .   Boris   Egorov

4. He is from _____ .   Russia   country

2 Match. Write the letter.

IDENTIFICATION

FIRST NAME:: **Pamela**

LAST NAME: **Reese**

COUNTRY: **United States**

1. __c__ What's her name?   a. Reese

2. ____ What's her last name?   b. the United States

3. ____ What's her first name?   c. Pamela Reese

4. ____ Where is she from?   d. Pamela

3 **Complete the calendar.**

JANUARY	February		APRIL
1 2 3 4 5	1 2	1	1 2 3 4 5
6 7 8 9 10 11 12	3 4 5 6 7 8 9	2 3 4 5 6 7 8	6 7 8 9 10 11 12
13 14 15 16 17 18 19	10 11 12 13 14 15 16	9 10 11 12 13 14 15	13 14 15 16 17 18 19
20 21 22 23 24 25 26	17 18 19 20 21 22 23	16 17 18 19 20 21 22	20 21 22 23 24 25 26
27 28 29 30 31	24 25 26 27 28 29	23 24 25 26 27 28 29	27 28 29 30
		30 31	

		JULY	
1 2 3	1 2 3 4 5 6 7	1 2 3 4 5	1 2
4 5 6 7 8 9 10	8 9 10 11 12 13 14	6 7 8 9 10 11 12	3 4 5 6 7 8 9
11 12 13 14 15 16 17	15 16 17 18 19 20 21	13 14 15 16 17 18 19	10 11 12 13 14 15 16
18 19 20 21 22 23 24	22 23 24 25 26 27 28	20 21 22 23 24 25 26	17 18 19 20 21 22 23
25 26 27 28 29 30 31	29 30	27 28 29 30 31	24 25 26 27 28 29 30
			31

	OCTOBER		DECEMBER
1 2 3 4 5 6	1 2 3 4	1	1 2 3 4 5 6
7 8 9 10 11 12 13	5 6 7 8 9 10 11	2 3 4 5 6 7 8	7 8 9 10 11 12 13
14 15 16 17 18 19 20	12 13 14 15 16 17 18	9 10 11 12 13 14 15	14 15 16 17 18 19 20
21 22 23 24 25 26 27	19 20 21 22 23 24 25	16 17 18 19 20 21 22	21 22 23 24 25 26 27
28 29 30 31	26 27 28 29 30 31	23 24 25 26 27 28 29	28 29 30 31
		30 31	

4 **Read. Write the answers. Then listen.**

Birthdays

In Group 1

January: *Lynn*   February: *Diego*
April: *Tony*   June: *Jim*   July: *Tina*

1. When is Jim's birthday? <u>   In June   </u>.

2. When is Lynn's birthday? <u>   </u>.

3. When is Diego's birthday? <u>   </u>.

4. When is Tony's birthday? <u>   </u>.

5. When is Tina's birthday? <u>   </u>.

Lesson E Writing

1 Complete the words.

> area code   first name   phone number
> country   last name

1. c __o__ __u__ __n__ __t__ __r__ __y__

2. a ___ ___ ___   c ___ ___ ___

3. f ___ ___ ___ ___   n ___ ___ ___

4. p ___ ___ ___   n ___ ___ ___ ___ ___

5. l ___ ___ ___   n ___ ___ ___

2 Look at the ID card. Complete the sentences.

1. Her ___ first ___ ___ name ___ is Mei.

2. Her _____ _____ is Wu.

3. Her _____ _____ is 773.

4. Her _____ _____ is 555-1173.

5. She is from _____.

3 **Look at the ID card. Complete the sentences.**

SPRINGFIELD LIBRARY

Emma	Harris
FIRST NAME	LAST NAME
(407)	555-6524
AREA CODE	PHONE NUMBER

1. Her first name is _____ Emma _____.

2. Her last name is _____.

3. Her area code is _____.

4. Her phone number is _____.

4 **Read. Complete the driver's license. Then listen.**

Meet the new student at River Valley Driving School. His first name is Octavio. His last name is Diaz. He is from Mexico. His area code is 206. His phone number is 555-3687. His date of birth is December 7, 1999.

INTERNATIONAL
DRIVER'S LICENSE

Octavio	
FIRST NAME	LAST NAME
DATE OF BIRTH	PLACE OF BIRTH (COUNTRY)
AREA CODE	PHONE NUMBER

Check your answers. See page 132. **UNIT 1** **15**

Lesson F Another view

1 **Read the sentences. Look at the form. Fill in the correct answers.**

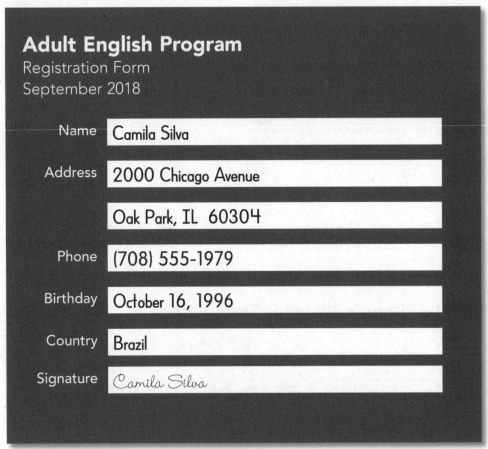

Adult English Program
Registration Form
September 2018

Name	Camila Silva
Address	2000 Chicago Avenue
	Oak Park, IL 60304
Phone	(708) 555-1979
Birthday	October 16, 1996
Country	Brazil
Signature	*Camila Silva*

1. Her last name is _____.
   - Ⓐ Park
   - Ⓑ Camila
   - ● Silva

2. Her area code is _____.
   - Ⓐ 60304
   - Ⓑ 708
   - Ⓒ 555

3. She is from _____.
   - Ⓐ Brazil
   - Ⓑ Chicago Avenue
   - Ⓒ October

4. Her first name is _____.
   - Ⓐ Camila
   - Ⓑ Silva
   - Ⓒ Oak

5. Her phone number is _____.
   - Ⓐ 555-1992
   - Ⓑ 555-1979
   - Ⓒ 555-2000

6. Her birthday is in _____.
   - Ⓐ Brazil
   - Ⓑ September
   - Ⓒ October

2 **Find and circle the words.**

1. country   c o c o u n t r y t e

2. name   m e n a m e a n

3. June   l J u l J u n e J y

4. month   m o n m o n t h t h

5. birthday   d a y b i r t h d a y b i

6. phone   p h p h o n e p n

3 **What is different? Cross it out.**

1.	Brazil	China	~~August~~	Mexico
2.	470	555-9832	212	201
3.	555-6782	555-1508	555-3744	972
4.	March	Somalia	October	July
5.	Vladimir	William	Russia	Rachel
6.	China	January	Mexico	Somalia
7.	May	September	December	Brazil

4 **Number the months in the correct order.**

_1_ January   ____ December

____ April   ____ March

____ August   ____ February

____ July   ____ October

____ May   ____ September

____ November   ____ June

January

Sunday	Monday	Tuesday	Wednesday	Thursday	Friday	Saturday
		1	2	3	4	5	6
7	8	9	10	11	12	13
14	15	16	17	18	19	20
21	22	23	24	25	26	27
28	29	30	31			

Check your answers. See page 132. **UNIT 1**   **17**

Lesson A Listening

1 Look at the pictures. Match.

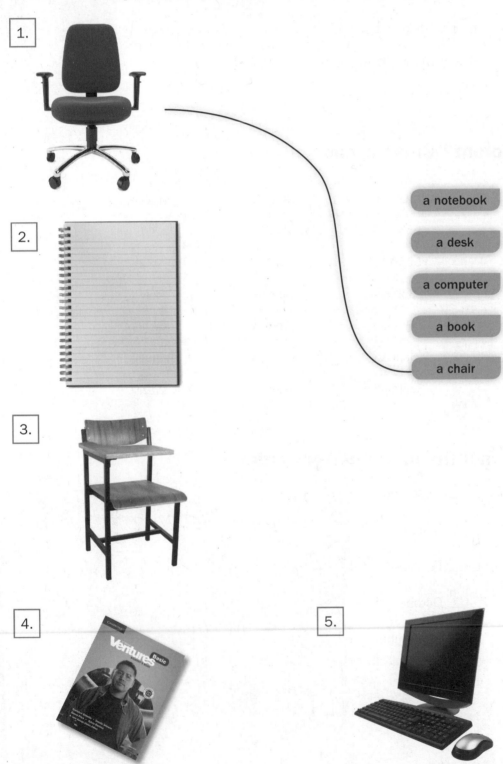

1.

2.

a notebook

a desk

a computer

a book

a chair

3.

4.

5.

2 Listen and number.

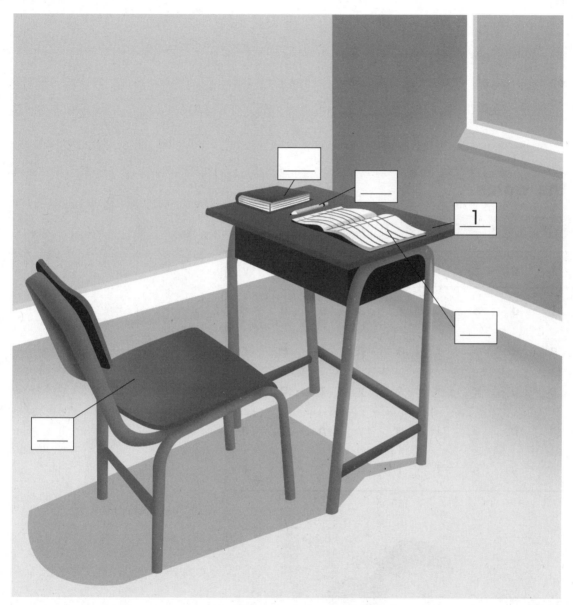

3 Complete the words.

1. b o o <u>k</u>
2. n o t e b o o ____
3. d e s ____
4. ____ o m p u t e r
5. p e n ____ i l
6. ____ h a i r

1 **Match.**

1. sta   ser
2. rul   per
3. diction   er
4. era   pler
5. pa   ary

2 **Find the words.**

| dictionary | eraser | paper | pen | ruler | stapler |

d	i	c	t	i	o	n	a	r	y
p	i	d	d	e	r	a	s	e	r
l	a	e	s	t	a	p	l	e	r
p	a	p	e	r	b	v	z	p	x
w	s	b	a	l	o	y	p	e	n
q	u	y	s	f	r	u	l	e	r

3 **Complete the words.**

dictionary eraser paper pen ruler stapler

1. d <u>i</u> <u>c</u> <u>t</u> <u>i</u> <u>o</u> <u>n</u> <u>a</u> <u>r</u> <u>y</u>

2. p ___ ___ ___ ___

3. s ___ ___ ___ ___ ___ ___

4. p ___ ___

5. r ___ ___ ___ ___

6. e ___ ___ ___ ___ ___

4 **Look at the pictures. Write the words.**

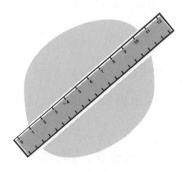

1. a _____

2. a _____

3. an _____

4. a _____

5. a _____

6. _____

Lesson C Where's my pencil?

1 **Look at the picture. Match. Write the letter.**

1. __c__ pencil   a. on the desk

2. _____ eraser   b. under the desk

3. _____ paper   c. in the desk

4. _____ dictionary   d. on the chair

5. _____ notebook   e. on the notebook

2 **Look at the picture in Exercise 1. Write _in_, _on_, or _under_. Then listen and check your answers.**

1. Where's my pencil?   _____In_____ the desk.

2. Where's my notebook?   _____ the chair.

3. Where's my dictionary?   _____ the desk.

4. Where's my paper?   _____ the desk.

5. Where's my eraser?   _____ the notebook.

3 **Look at the picture. Write the answers. Then listen and check your answers.**

1. **A** Where's my dictionary?

   B _On the desk_____.

2. **A** Where's my pencil?

   B _____.

3. **A** Where's my eraser?

   B _____.

4. **A** Where's my paper?

   B _____.

5. **A** Where's my notebook?

   B _____.

6. **A** Where's my ruler?

   B _____.

Check your answers. See page 132.

Lesson D Reading

1 Find and circle the words.

1. notebook	n o t (n o t e b o o k) t e
2. eraser	e r e r a s e r a s
3. computer	c c o m p u t e r t e r
4. pencil	e n p e n c i l i l p
5. desk	e s k d e s k d e n c i l
6. book	k o b o o o k b o o k

2 Read. Circle the correct sentences. Then listen.

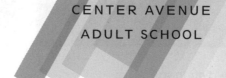

Dear Students,

Welcome to English class!
- You need a pencil.
- You need an eraser.
- You need a notebook.
- You need a dictionary.
- You need a ruler.

Thank you.

Your teacher,
Ellen

CENTER AVENUE
ADULT SCHOOL

1. (You need a dictionary.)
   You need a chair.

2. You need paper.
   You need a pencil.

3. You need a computer.
   You need a notebook.

4. You need a ruler.
   You need a stapler.

5. You need an eraser.
   You need a pen.

3 **Number the days in the correct order.**

_1_ Sunday

____ Friday

____ Monday

____ Wednesday

____ Thursday

____ Tuesday

____ Saturday

4 **Write the words.**

> Friday   Monday   Sunday   Thursday   Tuesday   Wednesday

```
                        S  _u_  _n_  _d_  _a_  _y_
          M  __  __  __  a  __
                        t
                        u  __  __  __
                        r  __  __  __
                        d  __  __  __  __  __
                        a
      T  __  __  __  __  __  __  y
```

5 **Write the days of the week.**

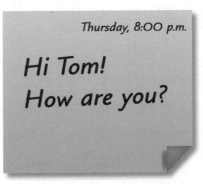

Thursday, 8:00 p.m.

Hi Tom!
How are you?

Tuesday, August 20

Dear Mom,

I miss you!

Love, Mary

postcard

1. **A** What day is it?

   B _____Friday_____ .

2. **A** What day is it?

   B _____ .

3. **A** What day is it?

   B _____ .

Lesson E Writing

1 **Look at the picture. Complete the sentences.**

| dictionary | eraser | notebook | pencil | ruler | stapler |

1. The _____notebook_____ is on the floor.

2. The _____ is on the chair.

3. The _____ is on the table.

4. The _____ is on the notebook.

5. The _____ is in the notebook.

6. The _____ is under the chair.

2 **Look at the picture. Write *in*, *on*, or *under*.**

What a mess! The dictionary is _____**on**_____ the chair. The stapler
                   1
is _____ the dictionary. The eraser is _____ the desk.
     2   3
The pencil is _____ the desk. The notebook is _____ the desk.
             4   5
The ruler is _____ the notebook.
         6

3 **Unscramble the letters. Match.**

1. c i p e l n   ruler

2. r a e r s e   notebook

3. u l r e r   dictionary

4. a p p r e   pencil

5. a r y d t c i o i n   eraser

6. t o o b k e n o   paper

4 **Write the words from Exercise 3.**

School Supplies for Class

1. I need a _____pencil_____ .

2. I need an _____ .

3. I need a _____ .

4. I need _____ .

5. I need a _____ .

6. I need a _____ .

Check your answers. See page 133. **UNIT 2** **27**

Lesson F Another view

1 **Read the sentences. Look at the class schedule.**
Fill in the correct answers.

RED ROCK ADULT SCHOOL CLASSES

MONDAY	TUESDAY	WEDNESDAY	THURSDAY
Computers 7:00–8:30 p.m.	**English** 6:30–8:00 p.m.	**Computers** 7:00–8:30 p.m.	**English** 6:30–8:00 p.m.

Computer Teacher: Sheila Brown **Room:** 206	**English Teacher:** Brad Ryan **Room:** 217

1. The English class is on _____.

   (A) Monday and Tuesday

   (B) Monday and Thursday

   ⬤ Tuesday and Thursday

2. The computer class is on _____.

   (A) Tuesday and Wednesday

   (B) Monday and Wednesday

   (C) Monday and Thursday

3. The computer class is in _____.

   (A) Room 106

   (B) Room 700

   (C) Room 217

4. The teacher on Monday and Wednesday

   is _____.

   (A) Brad Brown

   (B) Brad Ryan

   (C) Sheila Brown

5. The teacher on Tuesday and Thursday

   is _____.

   (A) Brad Ryan

   (B) Sheila Brown

   (C) Sheila Ryan

6. The English class is in _____.

   (A) Room 630

   (B) Room 217

   (C) Room 106

2 Complete the puzzle.

desk   dictionary   eraser   notebook   pen   pencil   ruler   stapler

Across →

1. 4. 5. 7. 8.

Down ↓

2.

3.

6.

Lesson A Listening

1 **Look at the pictures. Circle the correct words.**

1.

son   (grandmother)

2.

daughter   son

3.

grandfather   daughter

4.

father   mother

5.

father   grandmother

6.

mother   son

2 **Complete the words.**

1. s __o__ n

2. f ____ t h ____ r

3. m ____ t h ____ r

4. g r ____ n d m ____ t h ____ r

5. d ____ ____ g h t ____ r

6. g r ____ n d f ____ t h ____ r

3 Listen and number the picture.

4 Look at the picture in Exercise 3. Write the words.

1. <u>m</u> <u>o</u> <u>t</u> <u>h</u> <u>e</u> <u>r</u>
2. __ __ __ __ __ __
3. __ __ __ __ __ __ __ __
4. __ __ __
5. __ __ __ __ __ __ __ __ __ __ __
6. __ __ __ __ __ __ __ __ __ __ __

Lesson B Family members

1 Match.

1. sister ——— daughter
2. son   uncle
3. grandmother —— brother
4. husband   father
5. mother   grandfather
6. aunt   wife

2 Write the words.

> aunt   brother   husband   sister   wife

```
              m
   b   r      o    t   h   e   r
             t
___ ___ ___  h   ___ ___ ___ ___ ___ ___
             e
___ ___ ___  r
___ ___ ___ ___ ___
```

3 Circle the correct letters.

1. aunt and uncle   a.    b.

Anita   Rick   Michael   Emily

2. mother and father   a.    b.

Julie   Jason   Michael   Emily

3. brother and sister   a.    b.

Julie   Jason   Michael   Emily

4 Look at the pictures in Exercise 3.
Write the answers.

1. **A** Who is Michael?
   B Emily's ____brother____.

2. **A** Who is Emily?
   B Michael's _____.

3. **A** Who is Jason?
   B Michael's _____.

4. **A** Who is Julie?
   B Michael's _____.

5. **A** Who is Rick?
   B Michael's _____.

6. **A** Who is Anita?
   B Emily's _____.

Lesson C Do you have a sister?

1 **Look at the pictures. Circle the answers. Then write.**

1. **A** Do you have a son?
   B _No, we don't._
   Yes, we do. (No, we don't.)

2. **A** Do you have a brother?
   B _____
   Yes, I do.   No, I don't.

3. **A** Do you have a daughter?
   B _____
   Yes, we do.   No, we don't.

4. **A** Do you have a wife?
   B _____
   Yes, I do.   No, I don't.

5. **A** Do you have a grandmother?
   B _____
   Yes, I do.   No, I don't.

2 **Look and listen. Then write the answers.**

| daughter | husband | sister | son |

1. **A** Carla, do you have a _____sister_____?

   B Yes, I do.

   A What's her name?

   B Gabriela.

2. **A** Carla, do you have a _____?

   B Yes, I do.

   A What's her name?

   B Inez.

3. **A** Carla, do you have a _____?

   B Yes, I do.

   A What's his name?

   B Roberto.

4. **A** Carla, do you have a _____?

   B Yes, I do.

   A What's his name?

   B Alfredo.

Lesson D Reading

1 **Read. Write the words. Then listen.**

> ## My Family
>
> My name is Geraldo. This is my family. This is my father. His name is Hugo. This is my mother. Her name is Magdalena. This is my wife, Pilar. This is my daughter, Ramona.

daughter   father   mother   wife

1. _____wife_____

2. _____

3. _____

4. _____

Geraldo

Hugo

Pilar

Ramona

Magdalena

2 **Look at the story in Exercise 1. Circle the answers.**

1. Ramona is Geraldo's mother.   Yes   (No)

2. Pilar is Geraldo's wife.   Yes   No

3. Magdalena is Geraldo's mother.   Yes   No

4. Hugo is Geraldo's brother.   Yes   No

5. Ramona is Hugo's wife.   Yes   No

3 **Complete the chart.**

baby   boy   girl   man   teenager   woman

Male	Female	Male or female
boy		

4 **Circle the answers. Then write the answers.**

1. Pat is a mother. Pat is a _____**woman**_____.
   man   (woman)

2. Joe is a father. Joe is a _____.
   man   woman

3. Charles is a son. Charles is a _____.
   boy   girl

4. Debbie is a daughter. Debbie is a _____.
   boy.   girl

5. Sharon is a wife. Sharon is a _____.
   man   woman

6. Jimmy is a husband. Jimmy is a _____.
   man   woman

7. Nancy is a grandmother. Nancy is a _____.
   man   woman

8. Heather is 13 years old. Heather is a _____.
   teenager   baby

9. Mark is one year old. Mark is a _____.
   teenager   baby

Lesson E Writing

1 **Unscramble the letters. Write the words.**

daughter	grandfather	mother	sister	uncle	wife

1. i f w e _____wife_____

2. n u l e c _____

3. s s i e t r _____

4. o e m h t r _____

5. d t h r e g a u _____

6. g f r a t a d n r h e _____

2 **Write. Use the words from Exercise 1.**

1. aunt and _____uncle_____

2. brother and _____

3. son and _____

4. husband and _____

5. father and _____

6. grandmother and _____

3 **Look at the baby's family. Write the words.**

1. _____

2. _____

3. _____baby_____

4. _____

5. _____

4 Look at Viktor's family. Write the words.

brother   daughter   father   mother   son   wife

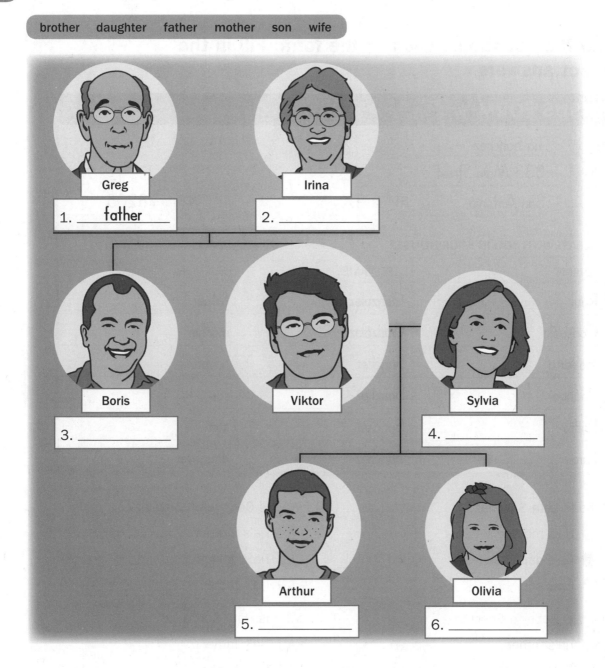

Greg
1. ____father____

Irina
2. _____

Boris
3. _____

Viktor

Sylvia
4. _____

Arthur
5. _____

Olivia
6. _____

5 Look at the picture in Exercise 4. Complete the sentences.

1. Viktor is Sylvia's _____husband_____.

2. Viktor is Irina's _____.

3. Viktor is Arthur's _____.

4. Viktor is Greg's _____.

5. Viktor is Boris's _____.

6. Viktor is Olivia's _____.

Lesson F Another view

1 **Read the questions. Look at the form. Fill in the correct answers.**

CENSUS FORM

NAME: Tia Sanchez

ADDRESS: 333 Main Street

CITY: San Antonio   STATE: TX   ZIP CODE: 78205

WHO LIVES WITH YOU IN YOUR HOUSE?

FIRST NAME	LAST NAME	RELATION
1. Raul	Gonzalez	father
2. Consuela	Gonzalez	mother
3. Roberto	Sanchez	husband
4. Rodrigo	Sanchez	son
5. Pedro	Sanchez	son
6. Lara	Sanchez	daughter

1. Who is Lara Sanchez?
   - Ⓐ Tia's mother
   - ● Tia's daughter
   - Ⓒ Tia's son

2. Who is Roberto Sanchez?
   - Ⓐ Tia's father
   - Ⓑ Tia's husband
   - Ⓒ Tia's son

3. Who is Pedro Sanchez?
   - Ⓐ Tia's father
   - Ⓑ Tia's husband
   - Ⓒ Tia's son

4. Who is Consuela Gonzalez?
   - Ⓐ Tia's mother
   - Ⓑ Tia's daughter
   - Ⓒ Tia's father

5. Who is Raul Gonzalez?
   - Ⓐ Tia's father
   - Ⓑ Tia's husband
   - Ⓒ Tia's son

6. Who is Tia Sanchez?
   - Ⓐ Roberto's mother
   - Ⓑ Roberto's daughter
   - Ⓒ Roberto's wife

2 **What is different? Cross it out.**

1.	aunt	woman	~~father~~	wife
2.	grandfather	son	husband	aunt
3.	daughter	son	wife	grandmother
4.	brother	uncle	aunt	man
5.	mother	brother	grandmother	daughter
6.	father	boy	grandfather	wife
7.	girl	man	aunt	woman

3 **Find the words.**

baby	husband	mother	sister	teenager	uncle	wife	woman

w	i	f	e	o	r	d	i	m	b	a	b	y	g
o	w	o	m	a	n	r	s	i	s	t	r	v	e
s	i	s	t	e	r	s	t	f	l	c	e	l	o
c	a	m	e	r	t	m	o	t	h	e	r	n	k
h	u	s	b	a	n	d	s	h	o	u	m	k	l
n	m	o	w	i	e	t	e	e	n	a	g	e	r
u	n	c	l	e	t	b	u	b	f	w	a	p	o

Lesson A Listening

1 **Look at the pictures. Circle the correct words.**

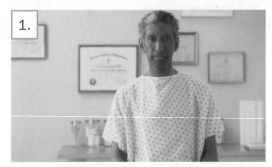

1.

(patient)

nurse

doctor

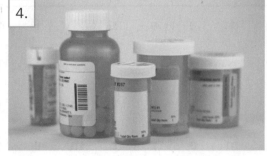

2.

nurse

doctor's office

doctor

3.

medicine

patient

nurse

4.

doctor

nurse

medicine

5.

medicine

doctor

patient

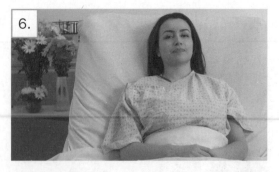

6.

doctor's office

nurse

patient

2 Listen and number.

3 Look at the picture in Exercise 2. Unscramble the letters.

1. 'srtdoco cfofei _____

2. snreu _____

3. tanipet _____

4. emdcneii _____

5. rodtco _____

Lesson B Parts of the body

1 **Complete the words.**

1. h __a__ n d   4. ____ r m

2. h e ____ d   5. l ____ g

3. f ____ o t   6. s t o m ____ c h

2 **Look at the pictures. What hurts? Write the words from Exercise 1.**

1. My ___stomach___!   2. My _____!   3. My _____!

4. My _____!   5. My _____!   6. My _____!

3 **Look at the pictures. Complete the sentences.
Then listen.**

1. **A** What's the matter?
   B My _____foot_____ hurts.

2. **A** What's the matter?
   B My _____ hurts.

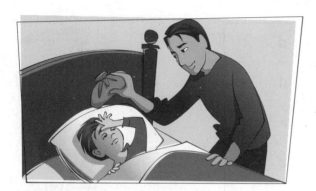

3. **A** What's the matter?
   B My _____ hurts.

4. **A** What's the matter?
   B My _____ hurts.

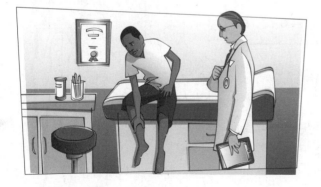

5. **A** What's the matter?
   B My _____ hurts.

6. **A** What's the matter?
   B My _____ hurts.

Lesson C My feet hurt.

1 Match.

1. eye   feet
2. hand   arms
3. foot   eyes
4. arm   hands
5. leg   legs

2 Find the words.

arms   eyes   feet   foot   hands   head   legs

r	e	p	l	e	g	s	t	u	r
f	q	b	o	p	h	a	n	d	s
o	u	m	j	f	e	e	t	k	e
f	o	o	t	t	l	s	c	z	j
t	e	r	h	e	a	d	z	y	e
a	r	m	s	c	o	m	u	t	r
l	e	k	f	t	p	e	y	e	s

3 **Look at the pictures. Complete the chart.**

	1	2
1. 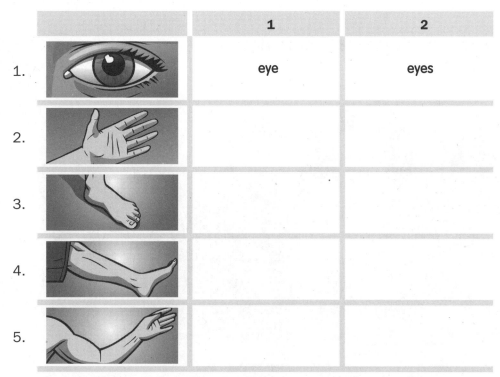	eye	eyes
2.		
3.		
4.		
5.		

4 **Look at the pictures. Write the words.**

1. **A** What hurts?
   B My ____legs____ !

2. **A** What hurts?
   B My _____ !

3. **A** What hurts?
   B My _____ !

4. **A** What hurts?
   B My _____ !

5. **A** What hurts?
   B My _____ !

6. **A** What hurts?
   B My _____ !

Lesson D Reading

1 **Look at the picture. Read and complete the sentences. Then listen.**

Where's the Doctor?

Five patients are at the doctor's office. The nurse is talking to the patients. Ruth's stomach hurts. Jun's arm hurts. Liliana's leg hurts. Omar's hand hurts. Tano's foot hurts. Where's the doctor? Doctor Han is not in his office. His head hurts. He is home in bed.

1. **Nurse** What hurts?
   Ruth My ___stomach___ hurts.

2. **Nurse** What hurts?
   Omar My _____ hurts.

3. **Nurse** What hurts?
   Tano My _____ hurts.

4. **Nurse** What hurts?
   Jun My _____ hurts.

5. **Nurse** What hurts?
   Liliana My _____ hurts.

6. **Nurse** What hurts?
   Doctor My _____ hurts.

2 **Look at the picture. Match. Write the letter.**

1. __c__ Ms. Simon   a. a cold
2. ____ Matt   b. a fever
3. ____ Ella   c. a headache
4. ____ Stefano   d. a sore throat
5. ____ Reyna   e. a stomachache
6. ____ Minh   f. a toothache

3 **Look at the pictures. Complete the sentences.**

1. I have a __toothache__.

2. I have a _____.

3. I have a _____.

Check your answers. See page 135.

Lesson E Writing

1 **Complete the puzzle.**

arm   cold   eyes   headache   legs   stomachache   sore throat   toothache

Across →

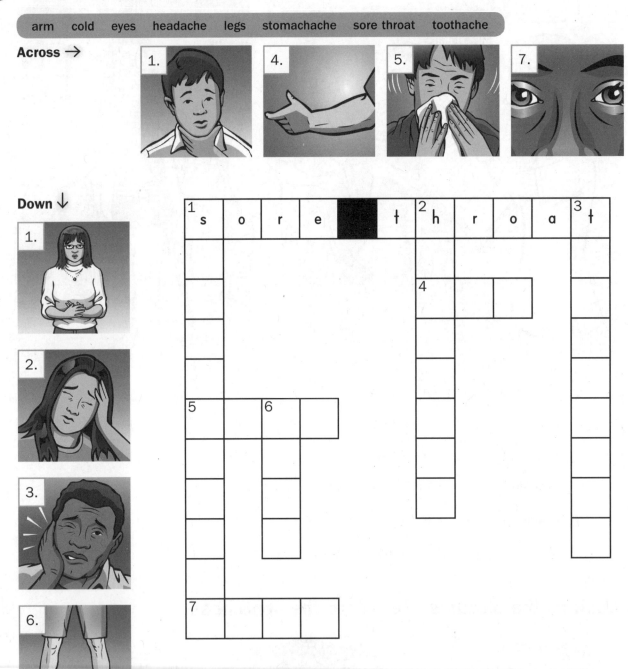

Down ↓

2 **Unscramble the letters. Write the words.**

cold   fever   headache   sore throat   stomachache

1. c l d o   cold
2. v r e e f   _____
3. d c h e a a e h   _____
4. o m a c s t h c e h a   _____
5. o r s e   o h r t a t   _____

3 **Read. Complete the sentences.**

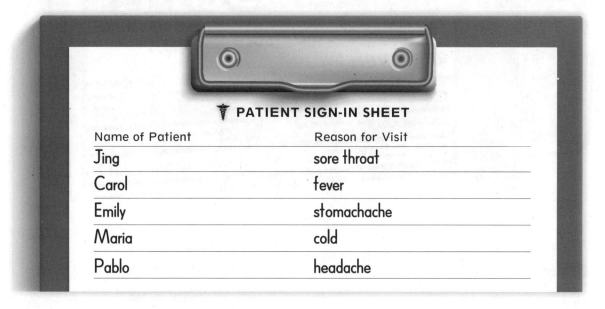

☤ **PATIENT SIGN-IN SHEET**

Name of Patient	Reason for Visit
Jing	sore throat
Carol	fever
Emily	stomachache
Maria	cold
Pablo	headache

1. Jing   I have a _____ sore throat _____.

2. Maria   I have a _____.

3. Pablo   I have a _____.

4. Emily   I have a _____.

5. Carol   I have a _____.

Check your answers. See page 135.

Lesson F Another view

1 **Read the sentences. Look at the label. Fill in the correct answers.**

1. This medicine is for a _____.
   - ● cold
   - Ⓑ toothache
   - Ⓒ stomachache

2. This medicine is for a _____.
   - Ⓐ headache
   - Ⓑ fever
   - Ⓒ toothache

3. This medicine is for a _____.
   - Ⓐ stomachache
   - Ⓑ sore throat
   - Ⓒ headache

4. Do not take this medicine _____.
   - Ⓐ after January 2017
   - Ⓑ after January 2018
   - Ⓒ after January 2019

5. This medicine has _____.
   - Ⓐ 20 tablets
   - Ⓑ 30 tablets
   - Ⓒ 50 tablets

6. This medicine is not for _____.
   - Ⓐ toothaches
   - Ⓑ fevers
   - Ⓒ colds

2 **Look at the picture. Write the words.**

1. _____hands_____

2. _____

3. _____

4. _____

5. _____

3 **What hurts? Look at the picture.**
Complete the sentences.

1. _____My head_____ hurts!

2. _____ hurts!

3. _____ hurts!

4. _____ hurts!

UNIT 5 AROUND TOWN

Lesson A Listening

1 **Look at the pictures. Match.**

1.

2.

3.

4.

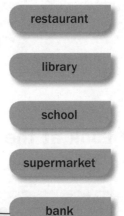

5.

restaurant

library

school

supermarket

bank

2 Listen and number.

a. ____

d. ____

b. ____

e. _1_

c. ____

3 Unscramble the letters. Write the words.

bank   library   restaurant   school   street   supermarket

1. s r e t e t   _____street_____

2. k a b n   _____

3. h c s l o o   _____

4. b l i r r a y   _____

5. t a u n r a t e s r   _____

6. m k t a r e p e r u s   _____

Lesson B Places around town

1 **Match. Then write the words.**

1. phar   station   _____

2. movie   macy   _____ pharmacy _____

3. gas   office   _____

4. post   tal   _____

5. laundro   mat   _____

6. hospi   theater   _____

2 **Find the words.**

> gas station   laundromat   pharmacy
> hospital   movie theater   post office

t	w	j	v	e	a	x	p	b	u	o	y	g	z
x	c	j	b	v	g	o	v	x	j	m	p	b	m
p	o	s	t	o	f	f	i	c	e	l	u	j	j
g	a	s	s	t	a	t	i	o	n	y	h	a	a
u	x	c	o	u	j	m	q	h	o	s	p	a	w
g	p	u	a	l	a	u	n	d	r	o	m	a	t
p	h	a	r	m	a	c	y	l	r	p	m	q	s
r	s	o	f	v	a	k	p	o	l	h	d	f	t
m	o	v	i	e	t	h	e	a	t	e	r	g	u
h	j	p	e	d	y	h	o	s	p	i	t	a	l
a	l	a	u	n	d	p	n	g	e	i	o	c	e

3 **Look at the pictures. Write the answers.**

gas station   laundromat   pharmacy
hospital   movie theater post office

1. **A** Where's Mark?
   B At the _____hospital_____.

2. **A** Where's Maya?
   B At the _____.

3. **A** Where's Jane?
   B At the _____.

4. **A** Where's Pavel?
   B At the _____.

5. **A** Where's Claudia?
   B At the _____.

6. **A** Where's Peter?
   B At the _____.

Lesson C The school is on Main Street.

1 Look at the picture. Circle the answers. Then write.

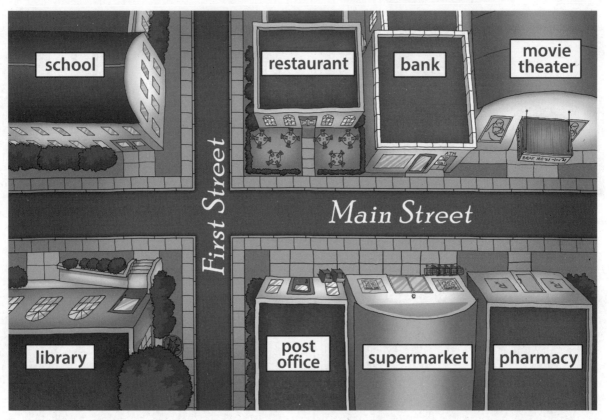

1. The pharmacy is _____**next to**_____ the supermarket.
   (next to) across from

2. The school is _____ the library.
   next to   across from

3. The supermarket is _____ the post office.
   next to   across from

4. The post office is _____ Main Street.
   on   across from

5. The bank is _____ the restaurant and the movie theater.
   across from   between

6. The restaurant is _____ the post office.
   between   across from

7. The library is _____ the post office.
   across from   at

8. The supermarket is _____ the pharmacy and the post office.
   across from   between

2 Look at the map. Write the words.

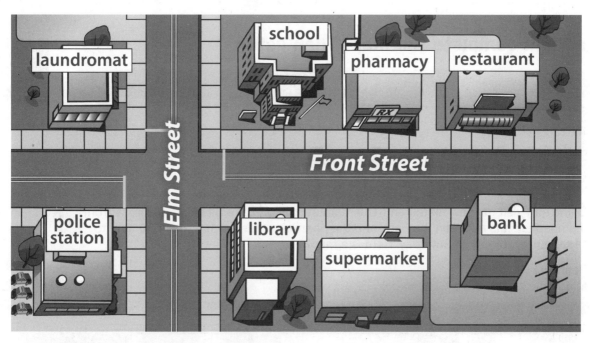

Across from   Between   Next to   On

1. **A** Where's the restaurant?

   B _____ Next to _____ the pharmacy.

2. **A** Where's the school?

   B _____ the library.

3. **A** Where's the pharmacy?

   B _____ the school and the restaurant.

4. **A** Where's the restaurant?

   B _____ Front Street.

3 Look at the map in Exercise 2. Match. Write the letter.

1. __c__ the laundromat   a. next to the pharmacy

2. _____ the supermarket   b. across from the laundromat

3. _____ the school   c. on Elm Street

4. _____ the library   d. between the library and the bank

5. _____ the police station   e. across from the school

Lesson D Reading

1 **Read and complete the map. Then listen.**

New Message

From: ming@cup.org
To: carey@cup.org
Subject: New Restaurant

Dear Carey,

Come and visit my new restaurant! The restaurant is on Lake Street. It is across from the hospital. It is between the bank and the pharmacy. It is open from 11:00 a.m. to 11:00 p.m., Monday to Saturday. Here is a map.

Best wishes,
Ming

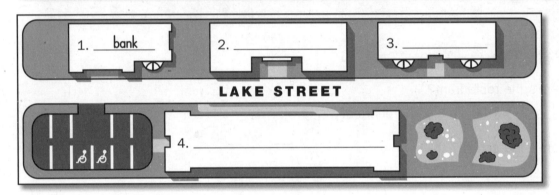

1. ___bank___   2. _____   3. _____

LAKE STREET

4. _____

2 **Look at the map in Exercise 1. Listen and write the words.**

1. **A** Where's the restaurant?
   B Across from the _____ hospital _____ .

2. **A** Where's the restaurant?
   B On _____ .

3. **A** Where's the restaurant?
   B Between the _____ and the _____ .

4. **A** Where's the bank?
   B Next to the _____ .

3 **Complete the words.**

bicycle   bus   car   foot   taxi   train

1. by c _a_ _r_

2. by t ___ ___ ___

3. by b ___ ___ ___ ___ ___ ___

4. by b ___ ___

5. by t ___ ___ ___ ___

6. on f ___ ___ ___

4 **Look at the picture. Complete the chart.**

Name	Transportation
Yoko	by taxi
Ted	
Martin	
Nadia	
Sam	
Katia	

Lesson E Writing

1 **Look at the picture. Write the words.**

bank   library   post office   school   supermarket

1. _____supermarket_____   4. _____

2. _____   5. _____

3. _____

2 **Look at the picture in Exercise 1. Complete the sentences.**

City School

The City School is on _____Third Avenue_____ . It is
                                                    1

across from a _____ . The school is between
                                2

the _____ and the _____ .
              3   4

A _____ is on Third Avenue, too.
        5

3 **Look at the map. Complete the sentences.**

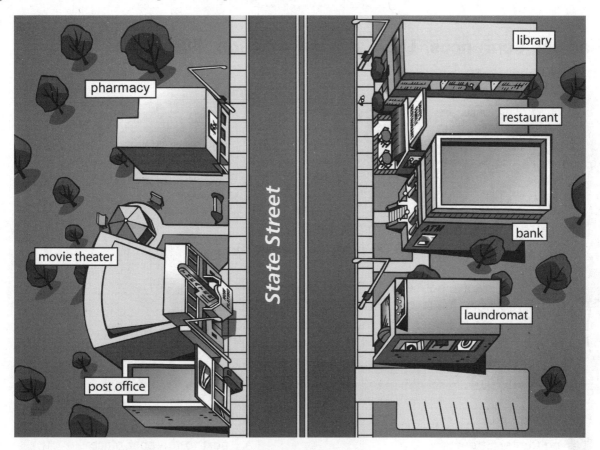

across from   across from   between   next to   on   on

STATE STREET MOVIE THEATER

The movie theater is _____**on**_____ State Street.
1

It is _____ a post office. A laundromat is
2

_____ the movie theater.
3

Dave's Family Restaurant is _____ State Street, too.
4

It is _____ the library and the bank. The restaurant is
5

_____ the pharmacy. See you at the movies!
6

Lesson F Another view

1 **Read the sentences. Look at the invitation. Fill in the correct answers.**

COME TO A PARTY

Where? At Binh's house
When? At 8:00 p.m. on Saturday

Binh's house is on Center Street. It is between the library and the post office. Binh's house is across from the supermarket. There is a movie theater next to the supermarket, too. The address is 259 Center Street.

1. Binh's house is _____ .

    ● on Center Street

    Ⓑ on Post Street

    Ⓒ on Market Street

2. Binh's house is _____ .

    Ⓐ between the supermarket and the post office

    Ⓑ between the library and the post office

    Ⓒ between the movie theater and the supermarket

3. The supermarket is _____ .

    Ⓐ next to Binh's house

    Ⓑ next to the post office

    Ⓒ across from Binh's house

4. The library is _____ .

    Ⓐ next to the post office

    Ⓑ next to Binh's house

    Ⓒ next to the supermarket

5. The movie theater is _____ .

    Ⓐ next to the supermarket

    Ⓑ across from the supermarket

    Ⓒ next to Binh's house

6. The post office is _____ .

    Ⓐ across from the movie theater

    Ⓑ next to the supermarket

    Ⓒ between the library and Binh's house

2 Find and circle the words.

1. bus   b a n k (b u s) s t r e e t c a r

2. taxi   t r a i n f o o t t a x i b a n k

3. train   t a x i b u s c e n t e r t r a i n

4. bicycle   l i b r a r y b i c y c l e f o o t

5. foot   c a r a c r o s s f o o t t a x i

6. car   s h o p c a r s t o r e p o s t

3 Listen and read. Complete the conversations.

| Excuse me | Next to the pharmacy | Thanks | Where's the supermarket |

1. **A** _____ Excuse me _____. Where's the laundromat?
   B On Maple Street.
   A Thanks.

2. **A** Excuse me. Where's the movie theater?
   B Across from Rosa's Restaurant.
   A _____.

3. **A** Excuse me. _____?
   B Between the bank and the library.
   A Thanks.

4. **A** Excuse me. Where's the bank?
   B _____.
   A Thanks.

Lesson A Listening

1 **Match.**

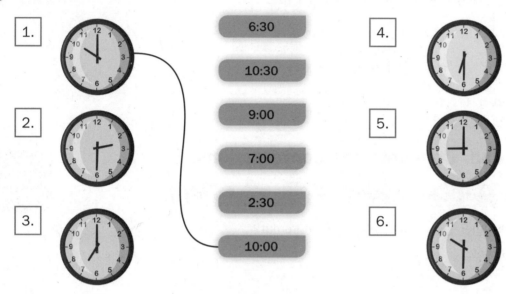

1.		6:30	4.
2.		10:30	5.
		9:00	
		7:00	
3.		2:30	6.
		10:00	

2 **Read. Write the time.**

TIME CARD		
DAY	**DATE**	**TIME IN**
Monday	May 12	2:30

1. _____2:30_____

TIME CARD		
DAY	**DATE**	**TIME IN**
Thursday	March 3	9:00

2. _____

TIME CARD		
DAY	**DATE**	**TIME IN**
Saturday	June 21	10:30

3. _____

TIME CARD		
DAY	**DATE**	**TIME IN**
Tuesday	July 8	7:00

4. _____

3 Listen and draw the hands on the clocks.

Lesson B Events

1 **Read. Write the answers.**

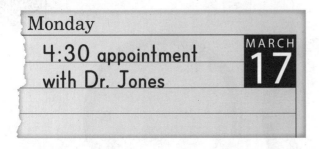

Monday

4:30 appointment
with Dr. Jones

MARCH
17

1. **A** What time is the appointment?

   B At _____4:30_____ on _____Monday_____.

Tuesday

3:30 meeting with
Dr. Kwan

MARCH
18

2. **A** What time is the meeting?

   B At _____ on _____.

Wednesday

9:30 movie with
Paco

MARCH
19

3. **A** What time is the movie?

   B At _____ on _____.

Thursday

5:00 class

MARCH
20

4. **A** What time is the class?

   B At _____ on _____.

2 **Complete the words.**

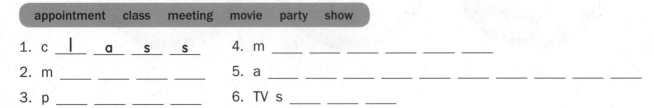

appointment   class   meeting   movie   party   show

1. c __l__ __a__ __s__ __s__   4. m ___ ___ ___ ___ ___

2. m ___ ___ ___ ___   5. a ___ ___ ___ ___ ___ ___ ___ ___ ___

3. p ___ ___ ___ ___   6. TV s ___ ___ ___

3 **Look at the pictures. Write the words.**

appointment   class   meeting   movie   party   TV show

1. **A** What time is the _____meeting_____ ?
   B At _____10:00_____ .

2. **A** What time is the _____ ?
   B At _____ .

3. **A** What time is the _____ ?
   B At _____ .

4. **A** What time is the _____ ?
   B At _____ .

5. **A** What time is the _____ ?
   B At _____ .

6. **A** What time is the _____ ?
   B At _____ .

Lesson C Is your class at 11:00?

1 **Look at the pictures. Write the answers.**

From: walker@cup.org

To: jones@cup.org

Dear Employees:

Our meeting is today at 11:00 a.m.

1. **A** Is the meeting at 12:00?
   B _No, it isn't. It's at 11:00 a.m._

ADMIT ONE
Love at Sunset
7:45 p.m.   Sat. 8/11/18
Theater 2

2. **A** Is the movie at 8:00?
   B _____

PARTY TONIGHT!
The Jam Club
Free Admission
8:30 p.m.

3. **A** Is the party at 8:30?
   B _____

CITY LIGHTS
Orchestra
JULY
19
SAT.
Seat K32
8:00 p.m.

4. **A** Is the concert at 6:30?
   B _____

Appointment Card

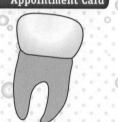

Your appointment:
3:30 p.m.
September 12

5. **A** Is the appointment at 3:30?
   B _____

2 **Look and read. Circle the correct answers.**
Then listen.

Monday, September 15			
8:30	Class	4:00	
9:00		5:00	Doctor's appointment ☹
10:00		6:30	
11:00		7:00	Movie with Louis
12:00	Lunch with Don ☺	8:00	
1:00		9:00	Birthday party ☺
2:00		10:00	
3:00	Meeting at work ☹	11:00	

1. Is the class at 8:00?   Yes, it is.   (No, it isn't.)

2. Is the appointment at 3:00?   Yes, it is.   No, it isn't.

3. Is the party at 9:00?   Yes, it is.   No, it isn't.

4. Is the movie at 6:30?   Yes, it is.   No, it isn't.

5. Is the meeting at 3:00?   Yes, it is.   No, it isn't.

3 **Look at the information in Exercise 2. Match.**

1. appointment   seven o'clock

2. meeting   eight-thirty

3. movie   five o'clock

4. party   three o'clock

5. class   nine o'clock

Check your answers. See pages 136–137.

Lesson D Reading

1 **Read and number the sentences in the correct order. Then listen.**

Mahmoud's Day

Mahmoud is busy today. His favorite TV show is at 7:30 in the morning. His doctor's appointment is at 10:30. His meeting with Abram is at 12:00. His English class is at 1:00 in the afternoon. His concert is at 5:00. His sister's birthday party is at 8:00 in the evening. What a day!

FROM THE DESK OF YOUR DOCTOR:

YOUR APPOINTMENT IS AT:
10:30 A.M.

LIVE Jazz
5:00 P.M.
SEAT 42C

ADMIT ONE

LIVE JAZZ
5:00 P.M. SEAT 42C
ADMIT ONE

_____ his sister's birthday party

_____ his doctor's appointment

__1__ his favorite TV show

_____ his concert

_____ his English class

_____ his meeting with Abram

2 **Look at the story in Exercise 1. Write the answers.**

1. What time is Mahmoud's appointment? _____ At 10:30 _____.

2. What time is Mahmoud's meeting with Abram? _____.

3. What time is Mahmoud's English class? _____.

4. What time is Mahmoud's favorite TV show? _____.

5. What time is Mahmoud's concert? _____.

6. What time is his sister's birthday party? _____.

3 Match.

a. in the evening   b. in the morning   c. at night   d. in the afternoon

4 Match. Write the letter.

1. __d__ 8:00 a.m.   a. in the evening
2. ____ 12:00 p.m.   b. in the afternoon
3. ____ 3:30 p.m.   c. at night
4. ____ 12:00 a.m.   d. in the morning
5. ____ 7:30 p.m.   e. at noon
6. ____ 11:00 p.m.   f. at midnight

5 Write the words.

| at midnight | at noon | in the evening |
| at night | in the afternoon | in the morning |

1. 6:30 a.m. _____in the morning_____
2. 2:00 p.m. _____
3. 10:30 p.m. _____
4. 12:00 p.m. _____
5. 6:00 p.m. _____
6. 12:00 a.m. _____

Lesson E Writing

1 Read. Complete the sentences.

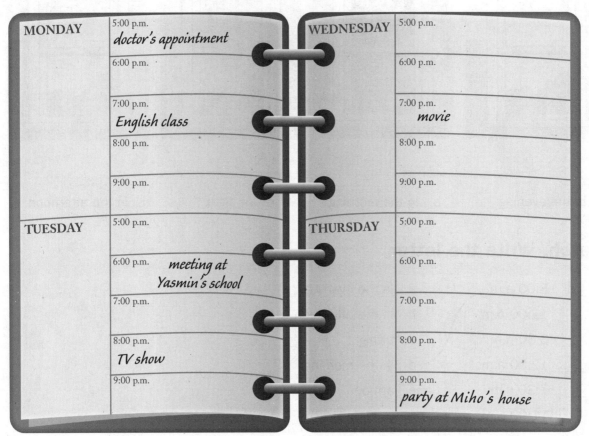

MONDAY	5:00 p.m. *doctor's appointment*		**WEDNESDAY**	5:00 p.m.
	6:00 p.m.			6:00 p.m.
	7:00 p.m. *English class*			7:00 p.m. *movie*
	8:00 p.m.			8:00 p.m.
	9:00 p.m.			9:00 p.m.
TUESDAY	5:00 p.m.		**THURSDAY**	5:00 p.m.
	6:00 p.m. *meeting at Yasmin's school*			6:00 p.m.
	7:00 p.m.			7:00 p.m.
	8:00 p.m. *TV show*			8:00 p.m.
	9:00 p.m.			9:00 p.m. *party at Miho's house*

1. **A** What time is the
   _____ party _____ ?

   B At 9:00 on Thursday.

2. **A** What time is the doctor's
   _____ ?

   B At 5:00 on Monday.

3. **A** What time is the
   _____ ?

   B At 8:00 on Tuesday.

4. **A** What time is the English
   _____ ?

   B At 7:00 on Monday.

5. **A** What time is the
   _____ ?

   B At 7:00 on Wednesday.

6. **A** What time is the
   _____ ?

   B At 6:00 on Tuesday.

2 Read. Complete the story.

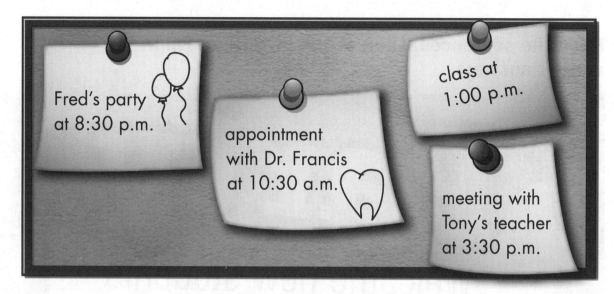

Jill is very busy today. Her _____**appointment**_____ with
                                       1

Dr. Francis is at 10:30. Her _____ is at 1:00.
                                       2

Her meeting with Tony's teacher is at _____ in the
                                       3

afternoon. Fred's party is at _____ in the evening.
                                       1

3 Complete the memo. Use the story in Exercise 2.

memo

Time:	Event:
10:30	appointment
_____	_____
_____	_____
_____	_____

1 **Read the sentences. Look at the invitation. Fill in the correct answers.**

Party

Welcome new students and teachers!
Saturday, August 3
8:00 p.m.
Where: Washington Adult School, 325 Main Street
RSVP: Alfonso Carillo, 555-6776

1. It's a party for _____.

   ● students and teachers

   (B) George Washington

   (C) Alfonso Carillo

2. The party is on _____.

   (A) Friday

   (B) Saturday

   (C) Sunday

3. The party is at _____.

   (A) 8:00 a.m.

   (B) 3:00 p.m.

   (C) 8:00 p.m.

4. The party is _____.

   (A) in the morning

   (B) in the afternoon

   (C) in the evening

2 **Use the code. Write the words.**

			Code			
1=a	5=e	9=i	13=m	17=q	21=u	25=y
2=b	6=f	10=j	14=n	18=r	22=v	26=z
3=c	7=g	11=k	15=o	19=s	23=w	
4=d	8=h	12=l	16=p	20=t	24=x	

1. 16   1   18   20   25
    _p_ _a_ _r_ _t_ _y_

2. 3   12   1   19   19

    ___ ___ ___ ___ ___

3. 5   22   5   14   9   14   7

    ___ ___ ___ ___ ___ ___ ___

4. 13   15   18   14   9   14   7

    ___ ___ ___ ___ ___ ___ ___

5. 13   9   4   14   9   7   8   20

    ___ ___ ___ ___ ___ ___ ___ ___

3 **Find the words from Exercise 2.**

m	e	l	a	p	p	o	n	o	b	o	m
i	n	t	e	v	e	n	i	n	g	f	o
p	a	r	t	y	l	i	s	h	z	a	v
i	n	g	w	e	n	c	l	a	s	s	p
g	m	o	r	n	i	n	g	i	n	o	r
c	o	n	c	m	i	d	n	i	g	h	t

Lesson A Listening

1 **Look at the pictures. Match.**

1.

4.

a dress

pants

2.

a shirt

5.

shoes

socks

3.

a T-shirt

6.

2 **Look at the picture. Write the words.**

a dress   a shirt   a T-shirt   pants   shoes   socks

1. a shirt
2. _____
3. _____
4. _____
5. _____
6. _____

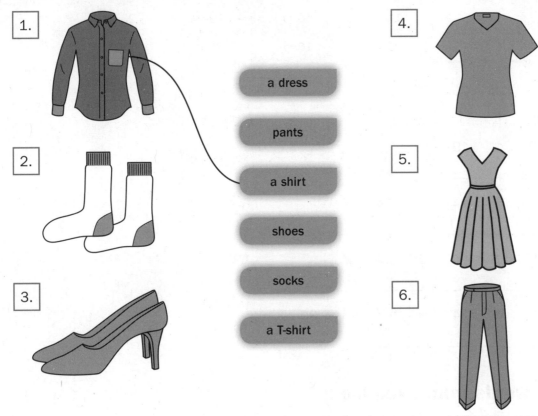

1.

2.

3.

4.

5.

6.

3 Listen and write.

dress   pants   shirt   shoes   socks   T-shirt

1. The _____shoes_____ are $39.00.

2. The _____ is $45.00.

3. The _____ are $10.99.

4. The _____ is $25.50.

5. The _____ is $40.99.

6. The _____ are $59.00.

4 Complete the puzzle. Use the words from Exercise 3.

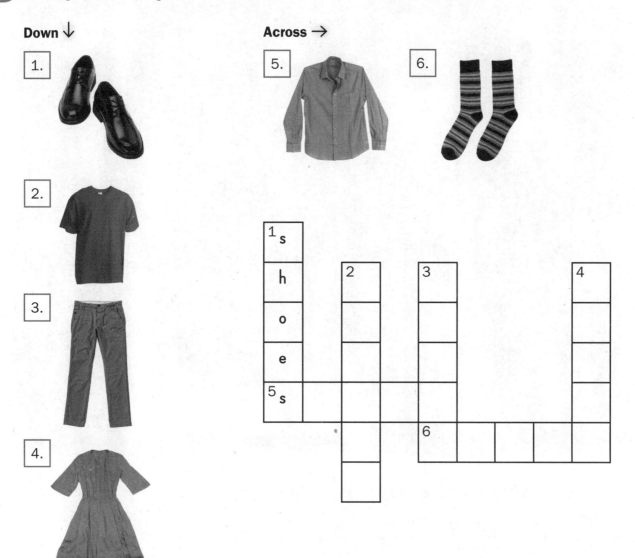

Down ↓

1.

2.

3.

4.

Across →

5.

6.

Lesson B Clothing

1 Complete the words.

blouse   jacket   raincoat   skirt   sweater   tie

1. a _t_ i e
2. a s w ___ ___ t e r
3. a s k ___ ___ t
4. a j a c k ___ ___
5. a r ___ ___ n c o a t
6. a b l ___ ___ s e

2 Complete the sentences. Use the words from Exercise 1.

1. The _____raincoat_____ is $49.95.
2. The _____ is $24.95.
3. The _____ is $59.95.
4. The _____ is $19.99.
5. The _____ is $19.95.
6. The _____ is $32.00.

3 **Read. Write the words and the prices.**

Clothing for your family. . .

$42.50

$29.99

$39.50

ON SALE NOW!

$25.99

$65.00

$24.50

1. The tie is _____ $25.99 _____ .
2. The _____ is $39.50.
3. The sweater is _____ .
4. The _____ is $29.99.
5. The skirt is _____ .
6. The _____ is $65.00.

Lesson C How much are the shoes?

1 **Read the questions. Circle the correct answers.**

1. How much are the _____?
   a. socks *(circled)*
   b. blouse
   c. tie

2. How much is the _____?
   a. shoes
   b. skirt
   c. socks

3. How much are the _____?
   a. tie
   b. skirt
   c. pants

4. How much is the _____?
   a. raincoat
   b. socks
   c. shoes

5. How much are the _____?
   a. tie
   b. sweater
   c. shoes

6. How much is the _____?
   a. shoes
   b. T-shirt
   c. pants

2 **Write *is* or *are*.**

1. **A** How much _____is_____ the tie?
   B $25.00.

2. **A** How much _____ the socks?
   B $1.99.

3. **A** How much _____ the blouse?
   B $29.99.

4. **A** How much _____ the pants?
   B $19.99.

5. **A** How much _____ the shoes?
   B $39.90.

6. **A** How much _____ the sweater?
   B $34.95.

3 **Look at the picture. Write *is* or *are* and the prices.**

1. **A** How much _____is_____ the blouse?

   B __$42.00__ .

2. **A** How much _____ the pants?

   B _____ .

3. **A** How much _____ the socks?

   B _____ .

4. **A** How much _____ the shirt?

   B _____ .

5. **A** How much _____ the sweater?

   B _____ .

6. **A** How much _____ the skirt?

   B _____ .

Lesson D Reading

1 **Read and circle the answers. Then listen.**

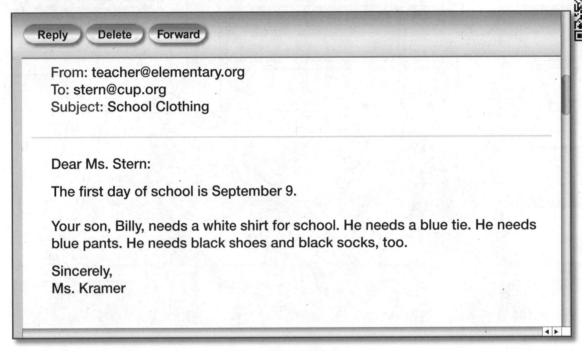

Reply   Delete   Forward

From: teacher@elementary.org
To: stern@cup.org
Subject: School Clothing

Dear Ms. Stern:

The first day of school is September 9.

Your son, Billy, needs a white shirt for school. He needs a blue tie. He needs blue pants. He needs black shoes and black socks, too.

Sincerely,
Ms. Kramer

1. Billy needs brown shoes.	Yes	(No)
2. Billy needs black socks.	Yes	No
3. Billy needs a blue tie.	Yes	No
4. Billy needs blue pants.	Yes	No
5. Billy needs a blue shirt.	Yes	No

2 **What color is the clothing in Exercise 1? Write the words.**

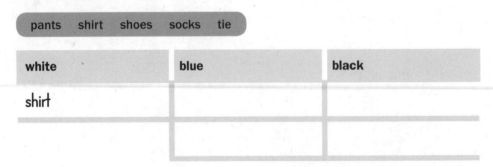

pants   shirt   shoes   socks   tie

white	blue	black
shirt		

3 **Look at the chart. Write the answers.**

Name	red	yellow	green	black	white	brown	blue
Sharmin			blouse	skirt			
Walter			tie	pants	shirt		
Lan		dress		shoes			
Omar	jacket					pants	sweater
Dora					blouse	shoes	skirt
Antonio	T-shirt	raincoat			socks		

1. **A** What color are Walter's pants?

   B _____Black_____ .

2. **A** What color is Lan's dress?

   B _____ .

3. **A** What color is Antonio's T-shirt?

   B _____ .

4. **A** What color is Dora's blouse?

   B _____ .

5. **A** What color is Sharmin's skirt?

   B _____ .

6. **A** What color are Dora's shoes?

   B _____ .

7. **A** What color is Omar's sweater?

   B _____ .

8. **A** What color is Walter's tie?

   B _____ .

Lesson E Writing

1 Complete the words.

1. __b__ __l__ o u s e

2. r a i n c ___ ___ t

3. j a ___ ___ e t

4. t i ___

5. s w e a t ___ ___

6. s k ___ ___ t

2 Look at the pictures. Write the words.

1. a _____blouse_____

2. a _____

3. a _____

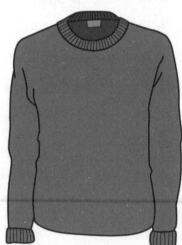

4. a _____

5. a _____

6. a _____

3 **Complete the chart.**

blouse jacket raincoat skirt sweater
dress pants shoes socks tie

Men's clothes	Men's and women's clothes	Women's clothes
	jacket	

4 **Read. Complete the shopping list. Then listen.**

Francesca is shopping today with her family. They need new clothes.

Her mother Carmela needs a dress. Her husband Mario needs a shirt. Her son Jerome needs pants. Her daughter Lisa needs a raincoat. Francesca needs new shoes.

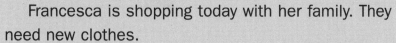

FRANCESCA'S SHOPPING LIST

NAME	CLOTHING
Francesca	shoes
Lisa	
Jerome	
Carmela	
Mario	

1 **Look at the picture. Complete the receipt.**

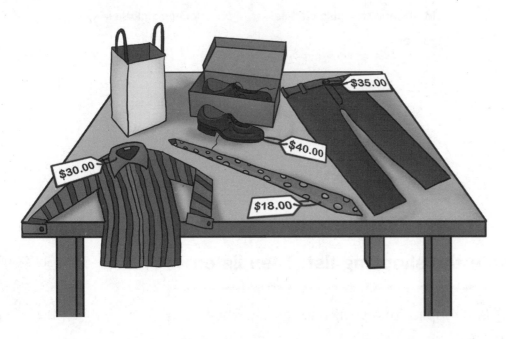

Sales Receipt

The House of Clothes

32 Park Street
New York, NY 10013
(212) 555-7736

Clothing

    tie $18.00

_____ $30.00

_____ $35.00

_____ $40.00

Total: . . . . _____

2 **Find the words.**

black   brown   orange   purple   white
blue   green   pink   red   yellow

s	w	e	s	h	o	j	a	c	r
p	r	i	n	g	r	e	e	n	d
t	e	c	y	e	l	l	o	w	g
k	a	t	h	r	e	d	l	n	o
b	l	a	c	k	m	b	l	u	e
c	o	l	s	c	h	o	b	l	u
s	h	a	w	h	i	t	e	r	o
a	i	n	c	t	s	h	i	b	l
n	m	p	b	r	o	w	n	e	c
r	o	r	a	n	g	e	s	o	c
p	i	n	k	d	r	e	p	a	s
o	u	s	e	p	u	r	p	l	e

3 **What is different? Cross it out.**

1.	shirt	blouse	~~pants~~
2.	jacket	shoes	raincoat
3.	shoes	T-shirt	socks
4.	skirt	dress	pants
5.	blouse	tie	dress

UNIT 8 WORK

Lesson A Listening

1 Complete the words.

1. m e c h a n <u>i</u> <u>c</u>
2. s e r v ___ ___
3. s a l e s p e r ___ ___ ___
4. r e c e p t i o n ___ ___ ___
5. c u s t o ___ ___ ___ ___
6. c a s h ___ ___ ___

2 Find the words from Exercise 1.

t	r	c	a	m	n	i	v	z	q	u	i
s	a	l	e	s	p	e	r	s	o	n	t
e	c	t	r	o	k	j	u	m	g	l	u
p	t	o	s	e	r	v	e	r	t	u	h
c	a	s	h	i	e	r	e	n	o	s	l
l	i	e	s	t	w	a	p	s	h	e	a
r	e	c	e	p	t	i	o	n	i	s	t
r	o	n	p	e	c	i	k	m	a	r	r
c	c	u	s	t	o	d	i	a	n	t	e
i	e	u	z	t	i	o	n	w	a	i	z
k	m	e	c	h	a	n	i	c	g	o	s

3 **Listen and number.**

Fatima
___

Edward
___

Gabriel
___

Cecilia
_1_

Bruno
___

Cathy
___

4 **Look at the pictures in Exercise 3. Match.**

1. Fatima   mechanic
2. Cecilia   cashier
3. Bruno   receptionist
4. Gabriel   custodian
5. Cathy   server
6. Edward   salesperson

Lesson B Job duties

1 Check (✓) the job duties.

Jobs	Sells clothes	Cleans buildings	Serves food	Answers the phone	Counts money	Fixes cars
server			✓			
mechanic						
salesperson						
receptionist						
custodian						
cashier						

2 Write the job duties.

> answers the phone   counts money   sells clothes
> cleans buildings   fixes cars   serves food

1. A server _____ serves food _____.

2. A receptionist _____.

3. A cashier _____.

4. A salesperson _____.

5. A custodian _____.

6. A mechanic _____.

3 Write the job duties.

1. _____ fixes cars _____   2. _____   3. _____

4 **Look at the pictures. Write the correct answers. Then listen.**

1. **A** What does she do?
   B She _____ sells clothes _____ .

2. **A** What does he do?
   B He _____ .

3. **A** What does she do?
   B She _____ .

4. **A** What does he do?
   B He _____ .

5. **A** What does she do?
   B She _____ .

6. **A** What does he do?
   B He _____ .

Lesson C Does he sell clothes?

1 **Look at the pictures. Circle the correct answers.**

1. Does he fix cars?
   a. Yes, he does.
   b. No, he doesn't.

2. Does she answer the phone?
   a. Yes, she does.
   b. No, she doesn't.

3. Does he clean buildings?
   a. Yes, he does.
   b. No, he doesn't.

4. Does she count money?
   a. Yes, she does.
   b. No, she doesn't.

5. Does he serve food?
   a. Yes, he does.
   b. No, he doesn't.

6. Does she sell clothes?
   a. Yes, she does.
   b. No, she doesn't.

2 **Look at the picture. Complete the sentences.**

1. **A** _____Does_____ Naoko ____serve____ food?

   B Yes, she _____does_____ .

2. **A** _____ Juan _____ money?

   B Yes, he _____ .

3. **A** _____ Imelda _____ the phone?

   B No, she _____ .

4. **A** _____ Franco _____ buildings?

   B Yes, he _____ .

5. **A** _____ Soo Yeun _____ cars?

   B No, she _____ .

6. **A** _____ Kevin _____ clothes?

   B Yes, he _____ .

1 **Read and complete the sentences. Then listen.**

Dear Mom,

   I have good news! The children have jobs for the summer.
In the morning, Nicolas is a mechanic. He fixes cars. In the evening, he is a
server. He serves food. Lydia is a cashier in the morning. She counts money. In
the evening, she is a salesperson. She sells clothes. In the afternoon, I am a
receptionist. I answer the phone. Our whole family is very busy!

   How are you? I miss you.

Love,

Tanya

1. **A** What does Lydia do in the evening?

   B She _sells clothes_____.

   She is a _salesperson_____.

2. **A** What does Nicolas do in the morning?

   B He _____.

   He is a _____.

3. **A** What does Lydia do in the morning?

   B She _____.

   She is a _____.

4. **A** What does Nicolas do in the evening?

   B He _____.

   He is a _____.

5. **A** What does Tanya do in the afternoon?

   B She _____.

   She is a _____.

2 **Look at the pictures. Complete the sentences.**

bus driver   painter   teacher's aide
homemaker   plumber   truck driver

1. **A** What does he do?
   B He's a _____ truck driver _____.

2. **A** What does she do?
   B She's a _____.

3. **A** What does he do?
   B He's a _____.

4. **A** What does she do?
   B She's a _____.

5. **A** What does he do?
   B He's a _____.

6. **A** What does she do?
   B She's a _____.

Lesson E Writing

1 Complete the words.

1. s e l l s <u>c</u> <u>l</u> o t h e s
2. c ____ ____ n t s m o n e y
3. ____ e r v e ____ f o o d
4. f i x ____ ____ c a r s
5. ____ ____ e a n s b u i l d i n g s
6. ____ ____ i v e s a b u s

2 Write the words.

| buildings   bus   cars   clothes   food   money   phone |

1. salesperson: sells _____<u>clothes</u>_____
2. server: serves _____
3. custodian: cleans _____
4. cashier: counts _____
5. mechanic: fixes _____
6. bus driver: drives a _____
7. receptionist: answers the _____

3 Look at the pictures. Complete the sentences.

1. She is a _____.
   She cleans ___<u>buildings</u>___.

2. He is a _____.
   He counts _____.

3. She is a _____.
   She drives a _____.

4 Look at the pictures. Complete the letter.

Dear Aunt Rose,

How are you? We are all busy and

happy. We have new jobs! Levon is a

_____server_____ at a restaurant on
        1

State Street. He _____

                              2

food. Tamar is a _____ .

                         3

She _____ a bus.

              4

I am a _____ . I

              5

_____ clothes.

        6

Write soon.

Love,

Rita

5 Complete the sentences. Use information from Exercise 4.

1. _____ sells clothes.

2. _____ is a bus driver.

3. _____ works at a restaurant.

1 Read the sentences. Look at the ads. Then fill in the
correct answers.

1. Job 1 is for a _____.

   ● server

   B plumber

   C receptionist

2. Job 2 is for a _____.

   A plumber

   B truck driver

   C receptionist

3. For Job 3, call _____.

   A 555-8743

   B 555-3370

   C 555-2192

4. For Job 2, call _____.

   A 555-8743

   B 555-3370

   C 555-2192

5. Job 4 is _____.

   A in the morning

   B in the evening

   C at night

6. Job 1 is _____.

   A in the morning

   B in the evening

   C at night

2 Write the words.

bus driver   cashier   mechanic   painter   plumber   server

_m_ _e_ _c_ h _a_ _n_ _i_ _c_
o
m
___ e ___ ___ ___ ___
___ l ___ m ___ ___ ___
___ a ___ ___ ___ ___ ___
k
___ ___ ___ ___ ___ e ___
___ ___ ___ ___ r ___ ___ ___

3 Look at the chart. Complete the sentences.

	drive a bus	count money	fix cars	drive a truck
Ted	✓			
Jessica				✓
Rashid			✓	
Irene		✓		

1. **A** What's Ted's job?
   B He is a _bus driver_ .
   A What does he do?
   B He _drives a bus_ .

2. **A** What's Irene's job?
   B She is a _____ .
   A What does she do?
   B She _____ .

3. **A** What's Rashid's job?
   B He is a _____ .
   A What does he do?
   B He _____ .

4. **A** What's Jessica's job?
   B She is a _____ .
   A What does she do?
   B She _____ .

Check your answers. See page 139.

UNIT 9 DAILY LIVING

Lesson A Listening

1 **Write the words.**

| bed | dishes | homework | laundry | lunch |

1. washing the   d   i   s   h   e   s
2. doing ____ ____ ____ ____ ____ ____ ____ ____
3. making ____ ____ ____ ____ ____
4. doing the ____ ____ ____ ____ ____ ____ ____
5. making the ____ ____ ____
6. drying the ____ ____ ____ ____ ____ ____

2 **Look at the pictures. Write the words.**

1. ____making lunch____   2. _____   3. _____

3 **Circle the words. Then write.**

1. _____washing_____ the dishes

   (washing) making

2. _____ lunch
   making   drying

3. _____ homework
   doing   washing

4. _____ the dishes
   drying   making

5. _____ the bed
   making   drying

6. _____ the laundry
   making   doing

Listen and number.

5 **Look at the picture in Exercise 4. Write the words.**

| doing homework | drying the dishes | making the bed |
| doing the laundry | making lunch | washing the dishes |

1. _____drying the dishes_____

2. _____

3. _____

4. _____

5. _____

6. _____

Lesson B Outside chores

1 **Unscramble the letters.**

1. n t c g i u t   ___cutting___   the grass

2. t n t i g e g   _____ the mail

3. k g n i a t   _____ out the trash

4. k w g l a n i   _____ the dog

5. r i n g t a w e   _____ the grass

6. h s w a g n i   _____ the car

2 **Look at the picture. Circle the chores.**

1. taking out the trash   (cutting the grass)

2. cutting the grass   taking out the trash

3. getting the mail   walking the dog

4. walking the dog   cutting the grass

5. watering the grass   walking the dog

6. getting the mail   washing the car

3 **Look at the pictures. Write the words.**

Cutting   Getting   Taking   Walking   Washing   Watering

1. **A** What is she doing?

   B ___Watering___ the grass.

2. **A** What is he doing?

   B _____ the grass.

3. **A** What is she doing?

   B _____ the mail.

4. **A** What is he doing?

   B _____ the car.

5. **A** What is she doing?

   B _____ out the trash.

6. **A** What is he doing?

   B _____ the dog.

Lesson C What are they doing?

1 Match.

1. drying   the bed
2. making   out the trash
3. getting   the laundry
4. taking   the dishes
5. washing   the dog
6. doing   the grass
7. cutting   the car
8. walking   the mail

2 Circle the correct answers. Write. Then listen.

1. **A** What _____ are _____ they doing?
          is   (are)
   B Getting the _____ mail _____.
          trash   (mail)

2. **A** What _____ he doing?
          is   are
   B Making _____.
          dinner   laundry

3. **A** What _____ she doing?
          is   are
   B Cutting the _____.
          dishes   grass

4. **A** What _____ they doing?
          is   are
   B Drying the _____.
          trash   dishes

5. **A** What _____ he doing?
          is   are
   B Walking the _____.
          dog   laundry

6. **A** What _____ she doing?
          is   are
   B Taking out the _____.
          trash   grass

3 Look at the pictures. Complete the sentences.

1. **A** What _____is_____ she doing?
   B ___Making___ the bed.

2. **A** What _____ they doing?
   B _____ lunch.

3. **A** What _____ she doing?
   B _____ the mail.

4. **A** What _____ they doing?
   B _____ the grass.

5. **A** What _____ she doing?
   B _____ the dishes.

6. **A** What _____ he doing?
   B _____ out the trash.

Lesson D Reading

1 **Read and circle the correct answers. Then listen.**

> The Gomez family is busy this morning.
> Bonita is washing the dishes in the kitchen.
> Magda is doing homework in the living room.
> Outside, Ramon is cutting the grass. Manuel
> and Leona are washing the car. Luisa is taking
> out the trash.

1. Bonita is doing homework.   Yes   (No)
2. Luisa is taking out the trash.   Yes   No
3. Magda is washing the dishes.   Yes   No
4. Manuel and Leona are washing the car.   Yes   No
5. Ramon is cutting the grass.   Yes   No

2 **Complete the sentences.**

1. What are Manuel and Leona doing?
   They are _____**washing the car**_____.

2. What is Bonita doing?
   She is _____.

3. What is Ramon doing?
   He is _____.

4. What is Magda doing?
   She is _____.

5. What is Luisa doing?
   She is _____.

3 **Look at the pictures. Write the words.**

bathroom   dining room   laundry room
bedroom   kitchen   living room

1. _____bathroom_____   2. _____   3. _____

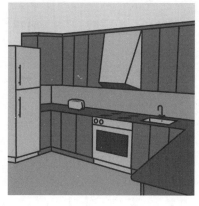

4. _____   5. _____   6. _____

4 **Circle the correct rooms for the chores.**

	Chores	Room	
1	drying the dishes	laundry room	kitchen
2.	making the bed	bedroom	bathroom
3.	washing the dishes	kitchen	bedroom
4.	doing the laundry	living room	laundry room
5.	making lunch	kitchen	bathroom

Lesson E Writing

1 Complete the words.

1. d __r__ __y__ __i__ __n__ __g__ the dishes

2. w ___ ___ ___ ___ ___ ___ the dishes

3. m ___ ___ ___ ___ ___ lunch

4. d ___ ___ ___ ___ homework

5. m ___ ___ ___ ___ ___ the bed

6. d ___ ___ ___ ___ the laundry

2 Look at the chart. Write the chores.

Chores	Sun	Min	Dae	Chul	Soo	Chin
do homework	✓					
make the bed			✓			
make lunch				✓		
wash the dishes						✓
dry the dishes					✓	
do the laundry		✓				

1. Sun is _____ doing homework _____.

2. Dae is _____.

3. Soo is _____.

4. Chin is _____.

5. Min is _____.

6. Chul is _____.

3 **Look at the picture. Complete the chore chart.**

Name	Chore
Justin	doing the laundry
Melissa	
Henry	
Penny	
Bill	
Erica	

Lesson F Another view

1 **Read the sentences. Look at the calendar.
Fill in the correct answers.**

Monday	Tuesday	Wednesday	Thursday	Friday
Erin	Adam	Andy	Suzy	Sara
beds	grass	car	laundry	trash

1. Today is Wednesday. Andy is _____.

   Ⓐ making the beds

   ⬤ washing the car

   Ⓒ cutting the grass

2. Today is Monday. Erin is _____.

   Ⓐ making the beds

   Ⓑ taking out the trash

   Ⓒ doing the laundry

3. Today is Thursday. Suzy is _____.

   Ⓐ cutting the grass

   Ⓑ making the beds

   Ⓒ doing the laundry

4. Today is Tuesday. Adam is _____.

   Ⓐ cutting the grass

   Ⓑ washing the car

   Ⓒ taking out the trash

5. Today is Friday. Sara is _____.

   Ⓐ making the beds

   Ⓑ doing the laundry

   Ⓒ taking out the trash

2 **Look at the calendar in Exercise 1.
Complete the sentences.**

1. It's Wednesday. Andy _____ the car.

2. It's Monday. Erin _____ the beds.

3. It's Friday. Sara _____ out the trash.

4. It's Tuesday. Adam _____ the grass.

5. It's Thursday. Suzy _____ the laundry.

3 **Unscramble the letters. Write the words.**

> bathroom   dining room   laundry room
> bedroom   kitchen   living room

1. b t h a o o r m   _____bathroom_____
2. r o m o b d e   _____
3. k c h n e t i   _____
4. n d i g n i   o r o m   _____
5. v i n g l i   m o r o   _____
6. y r d u n l a   m r o o   _____

4 **Write the rooms.**

1. making lunch   _____kitchen_____
2. doing the laundry   _____
3. drying the dishes   _____
4. making the bed   _____
5. washing the dishes   _____

5 **Complete the chart.**

> cutting the grass   making the bed   washing the dishes
> drying the dishes   walking the dog   watering the grass
> making lunch   washing the car

Chores inside the house	Chores outside the house
drying the dishes	cutting the grass

UNIT 10 FREE TIME

Lesson A Listening

1 **Complete the words.**

1. f __i__ s h
2. s w ____ m
3. d ____ n c e
4. e x ____ ____ c i s e
5. p l a y c ____ ____ d s
6. p l ____ ____ b a s k ____ ____ b a l l

2 **Find the words.**

| basketball | cards | dance | exercise | fish | play | swim |

b	i	c	y	t	a	b	l	s	h
p	d	a	n	c	e	y	z	f	i
e	x	e	r	p	l	a	y	m	b
e	x	e	r	c	i	s	e	d	o
c	a	r	d	s	m	o	n	w	t
e	y	f	i	s	w	i	m	y	a
d	a	v	n	g	e	l	u	s	w
n	c	f	i	s	h	i	m	b	a
b	a	s	k	e	t	b	a	l	l
d	s	z	o	n	f	r	e	x	p

3 **Listen and number. Then write.**

exercise   fish   play basketball   play cards   swim

1. _____swim_____

2. _____

3. _____

4. _____

5. _____

Lesson B Around the house

1 **Match. Then write the words.**

1. read ⎯⎯⎯⎯ in the garden
2. play   TV
3. listen to   the guitar
4. watch   magazines
5. work   music

_____read magazines_____

_____

_____

_____

_____

2 **Look at the pictures. Write the words.**

1. **A** What does she like to do?
   B Listen to _____music_____.

2. **A** What does he like to do?
   B Watch _____.

3. **A** What does she like to do?
   B Play _____.

4. **A** What does he like to do?
   B Work _____.

5. **A** What does she like to do?
   B Read _____.

3 **Look at the picture. Write the words.**

Cook	Play the guitar	Watch TV
Listen to music	Read magazines	Work in the garden

1. What does Sarita like to do? _____ Cook _____.

2. What does Steve like to do? _____.

3. What does Lola like to do? _____.

4. What does Marco like to do? _____.

5. What does Kaitlin like to do? _____.

6. What does Dennis like to do? _____.

Lesson C I like to watch TV.

1 **Write *like* or *likes*. Then listen.**

1. **A** What does she like to do?

   B She _____**likes**_____ to work in
      the garden.

2. **A** What does he like to do?

   B He _____ to play the guitar.

3. **A** What do they like to do?

   B They _____ to watch TV.

4. **A** What does she like to do?

   B She _____ to read magazines.

5. **A** What do they like to do?

   B They _____ to play cards.

6. **A** What do you like to do?

   B I _____ to cook.

7. **A** What does she like to do?

   B She _____ to play basketball.

8. **A** What do you like to do?

   B I _____ to play soccer.

2 **Look at the pictures. Circle _like_ or _likes_.**
Complete the sentences.

1. **A** What does he like to do?

   B He ___likes___ to ___exercise___ .

   like ~~likes~~

2. **A** What does she like to do?

   B She _____ to _____ .

   like   likes

3. **A** What does she like to do?

   B She _____ to _____ .

   like   likes

4. **A** What does he like to do?

   B He _____ to _____ .

   like   likes

5. **A** What do they like to do?

   B They _____ to _____ .

   like   likes

6. **A** What do they like to do?

   B They _____ to _____ .

   like   likes

1 **Read and circle the answers. Then listen.**

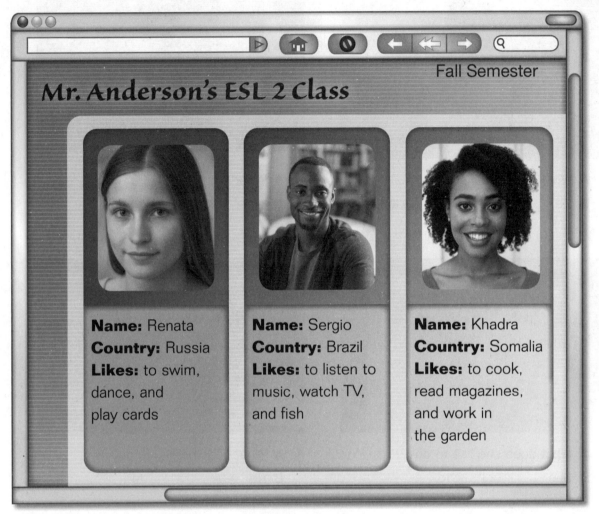

Fall Semester

Mr. Anderson's ESL 2 Class

Name: Renata
Country: Russia
Likes: to swim, dance, and play cards

Name: Sergio
Country: Brazil
Likes: to listen to music, watch TV, and fish

Name: Khadra
Country: Somalia
Likes: to cook, read magazines, and work in the garden

1. Renata likes to swim.	Yes	No
2. Sergio likes to cook.	Yes	No
3. Khadra likes to play cards.	Yes	No
4. Renata likes to work in the garden.	Yes	No
5. Sergio likes to watch TV.	Yes	No
6. Khadra likes to read magazines.	Yes	No

2 **What do they like to do? Look and match.**

travel

shop

volunteer

exercise

go to the movies

Lesson E Writing

1 Complete the words.

cook   dance   fish   shop   swim   volunteer

1. __s__ __w__ __i__ m
2. ___ ___ ___ h
3. ___ ___ ___ k
4. ___ ___ ___ p
5. ___ ___ ___ ___ e
6. ___ ___ ___ ___ ___ ___ ___ ___ r

2 Read. Complete the sentences.

	work in the garden	fish	volunteer	play cards	swim
Flor	✓				
Alvaro				✓	
Vera					✓
Brian		✓			
Kim			✓		

1. Flor likes to ___work in the garden___ .
2. Vera likes to _____ .
3. Kim likes to _____ .
4. Brian likes to _____ .
5. Alvaro likes to _____ .

3 Complete the sentences.

exercise   go   listen to   play   read   visit   watch

1. Jason likes to _____play_____ basketball on Saturday.

2. Jason likes to _____ TV on Thursday.

3. Jason likes to _____ magazines on Wednesday.

4. Jason likes to _____ to the movies on Sunday.

5. Jason likes to _____ friends on Friday.

6. Jason likes to _____ on Monday.

7. Jason likes to _____ music on Tuesday.

4 Write the information from Exercise 3
on the calendar.

Jason's Calendar

Sunday	Monday	Tuesday	Wednesday	Thursday	Friday	Saturday
1	2	3	4	5	6	7
						play basketball

1 **Read the sentences. Look at the catalog.**
Fill in the correct answers.

Community Center Classes
September 2 to December 12

Learn to dance!
Monday and Wednesday
11:00 a.m. – 12:30 p.m.
Room 110
$95.00

Learn to swim!
Tuesday and Thursday
9:00 a.m. – 10:30 a.m.
Pool
$100.00

Learn to play basketball!
Friday
2:30 p.m. – 4:30 p.m.
Room 115
$75.00

Learn to cook!
Monday and Wednesday
10:30 a.m. – 12:00 p.m.
Room 121
$85.00

1. The dance class is in Room _____.
   - ● 110
   - B 115
   - C 121

2. The cooking class is in Room _____.
   - A 110
   - B 115
   - C 121

3. The basketball class is _____.
   - A in the morning
   - B in the afternoon
   - C in the evening

4. The swimming class is _____.
   - A in the morning
   - B in the afternoon
   - C in the evening

5. The dance class is _____.
   - A $85.00
   - B $95.00
   - C $100.00

6. The basketball class is _____.
   - A $75.00
   - B $85.00
   - C $100.00

2 **Unscramble the letters. Write the words.**

| listen to music | play cards | read magazines |
| play basketball | play the guitar | visit friends |

1. y a p l   d s a r c   _____ play cards _____

2. s i t v i   f i r n e s d   _____

3. a y l p   e h t   t r a i u g   _____

4. a e d r   g z a m n i e a s   _____

5. l y a p   k b l s e t a a l b   _____

6. n e t s l i   o t   c s i u m   _____

3 **Complete the chart.**

| go to the movies | run | shop | travel | visit friends | volunteer |

Costs money $$$	Costs no money ~~$$$~~
travel	

4 **Complete the chart.**

| dance | listen to music | play cards | read magazines | swim |
| go online | play basketball | play soccer | run | watch TV |

Exercise	No exercise
dance	

REFERENCE

Possessive adjectives

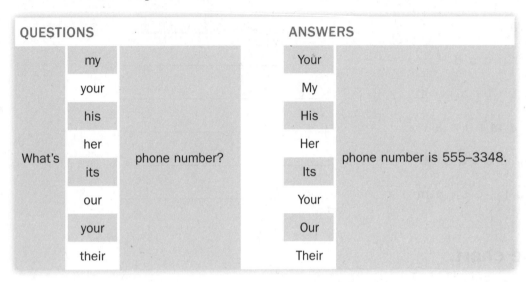

QUESTIONS			ANSWERS		
	my		Your		
	your		My		
	his		His		
What's	her	phone number?	Her	phone number is 555–3348.
	its		Its		
	our		Your		
	your		Our		
	their		Their		

Present of *be*

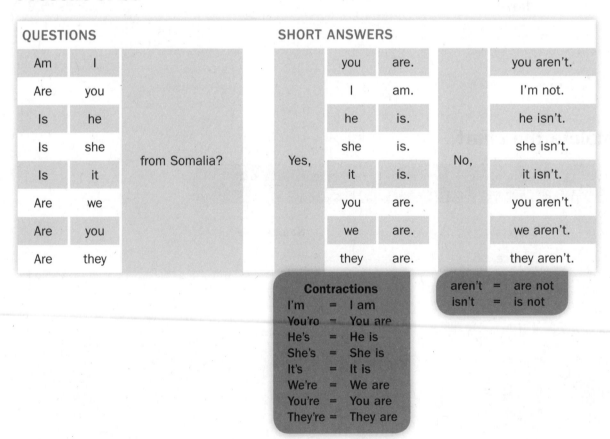

QUESTIONS			SHORT ANSWERS					
Am	I			you	are.		you aren't.	
Are	you			I	am.		I'm not.	
Is	he			he	is.		he isn't.	
Is	she	from Somalia?	Yes,	she	is.	No,	she isn't.	
Is	it			it	is.		it isn't.	
Are	we			you	are.		you aren't.	
Are	you			we	are.		we aren't.	
Are	they			they	are.		they aren't.	

Contractions

I'm	=	I am
You'ro	=	You are
He's	=	He is
She's	=	She is
It's	=	It is
We're	=	We are
You're	=	You are
They're	=	They are

aren't	=	are not
isn't	=	is not

Simple present

Do	I			you	do.			you	don't.
Do	you			I	do.			I	don't.
Does	he			he	does.			he	doesn't.
Does	she	sell clothes?	Yes,	she	does.	No,		she	doesn't.
Does	it			it	does.			it	doesn't.
Do	we			you	do.			you	don't.
Do	you			we	do.			we	don't.
Do	they			they	do.			they	don't.

SHORT ANSWERS

don't = do not
doesn't = does not

Present continuous

QUESTIONS WITH *WHAT* SHORT ANSWERS

What	am	I		
	are	you		
	is	he		
	is	she	doing?	Working.
	is	it		
	are	we		
	are	you		
	are	they		

Simple present of *like to* + verb

QUESTIONS WITH *WHAT*

What	do	I	like to do?
	do	you	
	does	he	
	does	she	
	does	it	
	do	we	
	do	you	
	do	they	

ANSWERS

You	like	to swim.
I	like	
He	likes	
She	likes	
It	likes	
You	like	
We	like	
They	like	

YES / NO QUESTIONS

Do	I	like to swim?
Do	you	
Does	he	
Does	she	
Does	it	
Do	we	
Do	you	
Do	they	

SHORT ANSWERS

Yes,	you	do.	No,	you	don't.
	I	do.		I	don't.
	he	does.		he	doesn't.
	she	does.		she	doesn't.
	it	does.		it	doesn't.
	you	do.		you	don't.
	we	do.		we	don't.
	they	do.		they	don't.

Simple present of *have*

Do	I	
Do	you	
Does	he	
Does	she	have a sister?
Do	we	
Do	you	
Do	they	

SHORT ANSWERS

	you	do.		you	don't.
	I	do.		I	don't.
	he	does.		he	doesn't.
Yes,	she	does.	No,	she	doesn't.
	you	do.		you	don't.
	we	do.		we	don't.
	they	do.		they	don't.

AFFIRMATIVE STATEMENTS

I	have	
You	have	
He	has	
She	has	a sister.
We	have	
You	have	
They	have	

NEGATIVE STATEMENTS

I	don't		
You	don't		
He	doesn't		
She	doesn't	have	a sister.
We	don't		
You	don't		
They	don't		

Capitalization rules

Begin the first word in a sentence or question with a capital letter.	**M**y name is Nancy. **W**here is Ivan from?
Begin the names of months and days of the week with a capital letter.	**J**anuary **S**unday
Begin the names of countries, states/provinces, cities, streets, and other places with a capital letter.	**M**exico **F**lorida **T**ampa **P**ine **A**venue **T**he **C**lothes **P**lace
Begin the names of people with a capital letter.	**S**ara **G**arza **E**rnesto **D**elgado
Begin family relationship words with a capital when they are part of a name. Do not begin family relationship words with a capital when they are not part of a name.	I like **U**ncle Eduardo. My uncle is Eduardo.
Begin a title with a capital when it is part of the name.	**M**rs. Navarro **D**r. Martin

Punctuation rules

Use a period to end a sentence.	My name is Nancy.
Use a question mark at the end of a question.	What's your name?
Use an exclamation point to show emotion, emphasis, or surprise. It replaces a period.	It's Monday, your first day of English class! I love my family!
Use commas after the salutation and closing of a note, letter, or email.	Dear Grandma, Love, Meg
Use an apostrophe + an s to show possession.	the doctor's office = the office of the doctor Maria's son = the son of Maria a teacher's aide = an aide for a teacher

ANSWER KEY

Welcome

Exercise 1 page 2

D, H, L, P, T, X

Exercise 2 page 2

c, f, i, l, o, r, u, x

Exercise 3 page 3

a. 1   d. 3   g. 4
b. 6   e. 9   h. 7
c. 5   f. 8   i. 2

Exercise 4 page 4

1, 4, 7, 10, 13, 16, 19

Exercise 5 page 4

one, three, five, seven, nine, twelve, fourteen, sixteen, eighteen, twenty

Exercise 6 page 5

1. four   5. two
2. one   6. five
3. three   7. six
4. eight   8. seven

Unit 1: Personal information

Lesson A: Listening

Exercise 1 page 6

1. first name
2. last name
3. country
4. area code
5. phone number

Exercise 2 page 6

1. Anna
2. Lopez
3. Mexico
4. 254
5. 555-2992

Exercise 3 page 7

1. first name – Marta
2. last name – Zaya
3. phone number – 555-2763
4. area code – 619

Exercise 4 page 7

1. phone number
2. area code
3. last name
4. first name

Exercise 5 page 7

1. first name
2. last name
3. area code
4. phone number

Lesson B: Countries

Exercise 1 page 8

1. f   3. e   5. b   7. h
2. a   4. c   6. d   8. g

Exercise 2 page 8

1. China
2. Brazil
3. Russia
4. Mexico
5. Somalia
6. Haiti

Exercise 3 page 9

1. Somalia
2. The United States
3. China
4. Brazil
5. Russia
6. Mexico
7. Haiti
8. Vietnam

Lesson C: What's your name?

Exercise 1 page 10

1. her   5. her
2. his   6. his
3. his   7. her
4. her   8. his

Exercise 2 page 11

1. your   5. your
2. My   6. My
3. your   7. your
4. My   8. My

Exercise 3 page 11

Manuel
Alvez
917
555-9845

Lesson D: Reading

Exercise 1 page 12

1. Boris Egorov
2. Egorov
3. Boris
4. Russia

Exercise 2 page 12

1. c   2. a   3. d   4. b

Exercise 3 page 13

February, March, May, June, August, September, November

Exercise 4 page 13

1. In June
2. In January
3. In February
4. In April
5. In July

Lesson E: Writing

Exercise 1 page 14
1. country
2. area code
3. first name
4. phone number
5. last name

Exercise 2 page 14
1. first name
2. last name
3. area code
4. phone number
5. China

Exercise 3 page 15
1. Emma
2. Harris
3. 407
4. 555-6524

Exercise 4 page 15
First name: Octavio
Last name: Diaz
Date of birth: December 7, 1999
Place of birth: Mexico
Area code: 206
Phone number: 555-3687

Lesson F: Another view

Exercise 1 page 16
1. C   4. A
2. B   5. B
3. A   6. C

Exercise 2 page 17
1. c o (c o u n t r y) t e
2. m e (n a m e) a n
3. l j u l (J u n e) J y
4. m o n (m o n t h) t h
5. d a y (b i r t h d a y) b i
6. p h (p h o n e) p n

Exercise 3 page 17
1. August   5. Russia
2. 555-9832   6. January
3. 972   7. Brazil
4. Somalia

Exercise 4 page 17
1: January   12: December
4: April   3: March
8: August   2: February
7: July   10: October
5: May   9: September
11: November   6: June

Unit 2: At school

Lesson A: Listening

Exercise 1 page 18
1. a chair
2. a notebook
3. a desk
4. a book
5. a computer

Exercise 2 page 19
(L to R:) 3, 5, 4, 1, 2
1. desk
2. notebook
3. chair
4. pencil
5. book

Exercise 3 page 19
1. book   4. computer
2. notebook   5. pencil
3. desk   6. chair

Lesson B: Classroom objects

Exercise 1 page 20
1. stapler
2. ruler
3. dictionary
4. eraser
5. paper

Exercise 2 page 20
(d i c t i o n a r y)
p i n d (e r a s e r)
l a e (s t a p l e r)
(p a p e r) b v z p x
w s b a l o y (p e n)
q u y s f (r u l e r)

Exercise 3 page 21
1. dictionary   4. pen
2. paper   5. ruler
3. stapler   6. eraser

Exercise 4 page 21
1. pen   4. dictionary
2. stapler   5. ruler
3. eraser   6. paper

Lesson C: Where's my pencil?

Exercise 1 page 22
1. c   3. a   5. d
2. e   4. b

Exercise 2 page 22
1. In   4. On
2. On   5. On
3. Under

Exercise 3 page 23
1. On the desk
2. Under the notebook
3. In the desk
4. On the floor
5. On the desk
6. On the chair

Lesson D: Reading

Exercise 1 page 24
1. n o t (n o t e b o o k) t e
2. e r (e r a s e r) a s
3. c (c o m p u t e r) t e r
4. e n (p e n c i l) i l p
5. e s k (d e s k) d e n c i l
6. k o b o o o k (b o o k)

Exercise 2 page 24

1. You need a dictionary.
2. You need a pencil.
3. You need a notebook.
4. You need a ruler.
5. You need an eraser.

Exercise 3 page 25

1: Sunday
6: Friday
2: Monday
4: Wednesday
5: Thursday
3: Tuesday
7: Saturday

Exercise 4 page 25

S u n d a y
M o n d a y
t
T u e s d a y
F r i d a y
W e d n e s d a y
a
T h u r s d a y

Exercise 5 page 25

1. Friday
2. Thursday
3. Tuesday

Lesson E: Writing

Exercise 1 page 26

1. notebook   4. eraser
2. dictionary   5. pencil
3. ruler   6. stapler

Exercise 2 page 27

1. on   4. in
2. on   5. under
3. on   6. in

Exercise 3 page 27

1. pencil   4. paper
2. eraser   5. dictionary
3. ruler   6. notebook

Exercise 4 page 27

1. pencil   4. paper
2. eraser   5. dictionary
3. ruler   6. notebook

Lesson F: Another view

Exercise 1 page 28

1. C   3. A   5. A
2. B   4. C   6. B

Exercise 2 page 29

Across
1. pen
4. dictionary
5. ruler
7. eraser
8. desk

Down
2. notebook
3. stapler
6. pencil

Unit 3:
Friends and family

Lesson A: Listening

Exercise 1 page 30

1. grandmother   4. mother
2. daughter   5. father
3. grandfather   6. son

Exercise 2 page 30

1. son   4. grandmother
2. father   5. daughter
3. mother   6. grandfather

Exercise 3 page 31

(L to R:) 1, 2, 5, 6, 4, 3

Exercise 4 page 31

1. mother
2. father
3. daughter
4. son
5. grandmother
6. grandfather

Lesson B: Family members

Exercise 1 page 32

1. sister - brother
2. son - daughter
3. grandmother - grandfather
4. husband - wife
5. mother - father
6. aunt - uncle

Exercise 2 page 32

m
b r o t h e r
a u n t
h u s b a n d
w i f e
s i s t e r

Exercise 3 page 33

1. a
2. a
3. b

Exercise 4 page 33

1. brother
2. sister
3. father
4. mother
5. uncle
6. aunt

Lesson C: Do you have a sister?

Exercise 1 page 34

1. No, we don't.
2. Yes, I do.
3. Yes, we do.
4. No, I don't.
5. Yes, I do.

Exercise 2 page 35

1. sister
2. daughter
3. husband
4. son

Lesson D: Reading

Exercise 1 page 36
1. wife
2. daughter
3. father
4. mother

Exercise 2 page 36
1. No
2. Yes
3. Yes
4. No
5. No

Exercise 3 page 37
Male: boy, man
Female: girl, woman
Male or Female: baby,
teenager

Exercise 4 page 37
1. woman
2. man
3. boy
4. girl
5. woman
6. man
7. woman
8. teenager
9. baby

Lesson E: Writing

Exercise 1 page 38
1. wife
2. uncle
3. sister
4. mother
5. daughter
6. grandfather

Exercise 2 page 38
1. uncle
2. sister
3. daughter
4. wife
5. mother
6. grandfather

Exercise 3 page 38
1. father
2. grandfather
3. baby
4. mother
5. grandmother

Exercise 4 page 39
1. father
2. mother
3. brother
4. wife
5. son
6. daughter

Exercise 5 page 39
1. husband
2. son
3. father
4. son
5. brother
6. father

Lesson F: Another view

Exercise 1 page 40
1. B
2. B
3. C
4. A
5. A
6. C

Exercise 2 page 41
1. father
2. aunt
3. son
4. aunt
5. brother
6. wife
7. man

Exercise 3 page 41

w i f e o r d i m b a b y g
o w o m a n r s i s t r v e
s i s t e r s t f l c e l o
c a m e r t m o t h e r n k
h u s b a n d s h o u m k l
n m o w i e t e e n a g e r
u n c l e t b u b f w a p o

Unit 4: Health

Lesson A: Listening

Exercise 1 page 42
1. patient
2. doctor's office
3. nurse
4. medicine
5. doctor
6. patient

Exercise 2 page 43
(L to R:) 1, 5, 2, 3, 4

Exercise 3 page 43
1. doctor's office
2. nurse
3. patient
4. medicine
5. doctor

Lesson B: Parts of the body

Exercise 1 page 44
1. hand
2. head
3. foot
4. arm
5. leg
6. stomach

Exercise 2 page 44
1. stomach
2. arm
3. foot
4. head
5. hand
6. leg

Exercise 3 page 45
1. foot
2. hand
3. head
4. stomach
5. leg
6. arm

Lesson C: My feet hurt.

Exercise 1 page 46
1. eye - eyes
2. hand - hands
3. foot - feet
4. arm - arms
5. leg - legs

Exercise 2 page 46

r e p l e g s t u r
f q b o p h a n d s
o u m j f e e t k e
f o o t t l s c z j
t e r h e a d z y e
a r m s c o m u t r
l e k f t p e y e s

Exercise 3 page 47
1. eye, eyes
2. hand, hands
3. foot, feet
4. leg, legs
5. arm, arms

Exercise 4 page 47

1. legs
2. arm
3. foot
4. hands
5. eyes
6. stomach

Lesson D: Reading

Exercise 1 page 48

1. stomach
2. hand
3. foot
4. arm
5. leg
6. head

Exercise 2 page 49

1. c   3. f   5. a
2. d   4. b   6. e

Exercise 3 page 49

1. toothache
2. headache
3. cold

Lesson E: Writing

Exercise 1 page 50

Across

1. sore throat
4. arm
5. cold
7. eyes

Down

1. stomachache
2. headache
3. toothache
6. legs

Exercise 2 page 51

1. cold
2. fever
3. headache
4. stomachache
5. sore throat

Exercise 3 page 51

1. sore throat
2. cold
3. headache
4. stomachache
5. fever

Lesson F: Another view

Exercise 1 page 52

1. A   3. B   5. C
2. B   4. C   6. A

Exercise 2 page 53

1. hands
2. eyes
3. feet
4. arms
5. legs

Exercise 3 page 53

1. My head
2. My stomach
3. My leg
4. My foot

Unit 5: Around town

Lesson A: Listening

Exercise 1 page 54

1. bank
2. library
3. restaurant
4. supermarket
5. school

Exercise 2 page 55

1. e   4. c
2. a   5. b
3. d

Exercise 3 page 55

1. street   4. library
2. bank   5. restaurant
3. school   6. supermarket

Lesson B: Places around town

Exercise 1 page 56

1. pharmacy
2. movie theater
3. gas station
4. post office
5. laundromat
6. hospital

Exercise 2 page 56

t w j v e a x p b u o y g z
x c j b v g o v x j m p b m
p o s t o f f i c e l u j j
g a s s t a t i o n y h a a
u x c o u j m q h o s p a w
g p u a l a u n d r o m a t
p h a r m a c y l r p m q s
r s o f v a k p o l h d f t
m o v i e t h e a t e r g u
h j p e d y h o s p i t a l
a l a u n d p n g e i o c e

Exercise 3 page 57

1. hospital
2. pharmacy
3. post office
4. movie theater
5. laundromat
6. gas station

Lesson C: The school is on Main Street.

Exercise 1 page 58

1. next to
2. across from
3. next to
4. on
5. between
6. across from
7. across from
8. between

Exercise 2 page 59

1. Next to   3. Between
2. Across from   4. On

Exercise 3 page 59

1. c   3. a   5. b
2. d   4. e

Lesson D: Reading

Exercise 1 page 60

1. bank   3. pharmacy
2. restaurant   4. hospital

Exercise 2 page 60

1. hospital
2. Lake Street
3. bank, pharmacy
4. restaurant

Exercise 3 page 61

1. car   4. bus
2. taxi   5. train
3. bicycle   6. foot

Exercise 4 page 61

Yoko: by taxi
Ted: by bus
Martin: by bicycle
Nadia: by car
Sam: on foot
Katia: by train

Lesson E: Writing

Exercise 1 page 62

1. supermarket
2. library
3. post office
4. school
5. bank

Exercise 2 page 62

1. Third Avenue
2. library
3. bank
4. post office
5. supermarket

Exercise 3 page 63

1. on
2. next to
3. across from
4. on
5. between
6. across from

Lesson F: Another view

Exercise 1 page 64

1. A   3. C   5. A
2. B   4. B   6. A

Exercise 2 page 65

1. b a n k (b u s) s t r e e t c a r
2. t r a i n f o o t (t a x i) b a n k
3. t a x i b u s (t r a i n) c e n t e r
4. l i b r a r y (b i c y c l e) f o o t
5. c a r a c r o s s (f o o t) t a x i
6. s h o p s t o r e (c a r) p o s t

Exercise 3 page 65

1. Excuse me
2. Thanks
3. Where's the supermarket
4. Next to the pharmacy

Unit 6: Time

Lesson A: Listening

Exercise 1 page 66

1. 10:00   4. 6:30
2. 2:30   5. 9:00
3. 7:00   6. 10:30

Exercise 2 page 66

1. 2:30
2. 9:00
3. 10:30
4. 7:00

Exercise 3 page 67

Lesson B: Events

Exercise 1 page 68

1. 4:30, Monday
2. 3:30, Tuesday
3. 9:30, Wednesday
4. 5:00, Thursday

Exercise 2 page 68

1. class   4. meeting
2. movie   5. appointment
3. party   6. show

Exercise 3 page 69

1A. meeting
1B. 10:00
2A. party
2B. 8:30
3A. class
3B. 11:00
4A. appointment
4B. 3:30
5A. movie
5B. 7:30
6A. TV show
6B. 9:00

Lesson C: Is your class at 11:00?

Exercise 1 page 70

1. No, it isn't. It's at 11:00 a.m.
2. No, it isn't. It's at 7:45 p.m.
3. Yes, it is.
4. No, it isn't. It's at 8:00 p.m.
5. Yes, it is.

Exercise 2 page 71

1. No, it isn't.
2. No, it isn't.
3. Yes, it is.
4. No, it isn't.
5. Yes, it is.

Exercise 3 page 71

1. appointment - five o'clock
2. meeting - three o'clock
3. movie - seven o'clock
4. party - nine o'clock
5. class - eight-thirty

Lesson D: Reading

Exercise 1 page 72

6: his sister's birthday party.
2: his doctor's appointment.
1: his favorite TV show.
5: his concert.
4: his English class.
3: his meeting with Abram.

Exercise 2 page 72

1. At 10:30   4. At 7:30
2. At 12:00   5. At 5:00
3. At 1:00   6. At 8:00

Exercise 3 page 73

1. d   2. c   3. a   4. b

Exercise 4 page 73

1. d   3. b   5. a
2. e   4. f   6. c

Exercise 5 page 73

1. in the morning
2. in the afternoon
3. at night
4. at noon
5. in the evening
6. at midnight

Lesson E: Writing

Exercise 1 page 74

1. party
2. appointment
3. TV show
4. class
5. movie
6. meeting

Exercise 2 page 75

1. appointment
2. class
3. 3:30
4. 8:30

Exercise 3 page 75

10:30 – appointment
1:00 – class
3:30 – meeting
8:30 – party

Lesson F: Another view

Exercise 1 page 76

1. A   2. B   3. C   4. C

Exercise 2 page 77

1. party
2. class
3. evening
4. morning
5. midnight

Exercise 3 page 77

m e l a p p o n o b o m
i n t e v e n i n g f o
p a r t y l i s h z a v
i n g w e n c l a s s p
g m o r n i n g i n o r
c o n c m i d n i g h t

Unit 7: Shopping

Lesson A: Listening

Exercise 1 page 78

1. a shirt   4. a T-shirt
2. socks   5. a dress
3. shoes   6. pants

Exercise 2 page 78

1. a shirt   4. pants
2. a T-shirt 5. socks
3. a dress   6. shoes

Exercise 3 page 79

1. shoes   4. T-shirt
2. dress   5. shirt
3. socks   6. pants

Exercise 4 page 79

Down	Across
1. shoes	5. shirt
2. T-shirt	6. socks
3. pants	
4. dress	

Lesson B: Clothing

Exercise 1 page 80

1. a tie   4. a jacket
2. a sweater   5. a raincoat
3. a skirt   6. a blouse

Exercise 2 page 80

1. raincoat   4. blouse
2. skirt   5. tie
3. jacket   6. sweater

Exercise 3 page 81

1. $25.99   4. blouse
2. raincoat 5. $24.50
3. $42.50   6. jacket

Lesson C: How much are the shoes?

Exercise 1 page 82

1. a   3. c   5. c
2. b   4. a   6. b

Exercise 2 page 82

1. is   4. are
2. are   5. are
3. is   6. is

Exercise 3 page 83

1A. is   4A. is
1B. $42.00   4B. $36.50
2A. are   5A. is
2B. $45.00   5B. $35.00
3A. are   6A. is
3B. $3.50   6B. $27.50

Lesson D: Reading

Exercise 1 page 84

1. No
2. Yes
3. Yes
4. Yes
5. No

Exercise 2 page 84

white: shirt
blue: pants, tie
black: shoes, socks

Exercise 3 page 85

1. Black
2. Yellow
3. Red
4. White
5. Black
6. Brown
7. Blue
8. Green

Lesson E: Writing

Exercise 1 page 86

1. blouse
2. raincoat
3. jacket
4. tie
5. sweater
6. skirt

Exercise 2 page 86

1. blouse
2. tie
3. raincoat
4. skirt
5. jacket
6. sweater

Exercise 3 page 87

Men's clothes: tie
Men's and women's clothes:
jacket, pants, raincoat,
shoes, socks, sweater
Women's clothes: blouse,
dress, skirt

Exercise 4 page 87

Francesca: shoes
Lisa: raincoat
Jerome: pants
Carmela: dress
Mario: shirt

Lesson F: Another view

Exercise 1 page 88

Clothing
tie
shirt
pants
shoes
Total: $123.00

Exercise 2 page 89

```
s w e s h o j a c r
p r i n g r e e n d
t e c y e l l o w g
k a t h r e d l n o
b l a c k m b l u e
c o l s c h o b l u
s h a w h i t e r o
a i n c t s h i b l
n m p b r o w n e c
r o r a n g e s o c
p i n k d r e p a s
o u s e p u r p l e
```

Exercise 3 page 89

1. pants
2. shoes
3. T-shirt
4. pants
5. tie

Unit 8: Work

Lesson A: Listening

Exercise 1 page 90

1. mechanic
2. server
3. salesperson
4. receptionist
5. custodian
6. cashier

Exercise 2 page 90

```
t r c a m n i v z q u i
s a l e s p e r s o n t
e c t r o k j u m g l u
p t o s e r v e r t u h
c a s h i e r e n o s l
l i e s t w a p s h e a
r e c e p t i o n i s t
r o n p e c i k m a r r
c c u s t o d i a n t e
i e u z t i o n w a i z
k m e c h a n i c g o s
```

Exercise 3 page 91

Top row: 2, 4, 6
Bottom row: 1, 3, 5

1. salesperson
2. receptionist
3. custodian
4. cashier
5. mechanic
6. server

Exercise 4 page 91

1. Fatima - receptionist
2. Cecilia - salesperson
3. Bruno - custodian
4. Gabriel - server
5. Cathy - mechanic
6. Edward - cashier

Lesson B: Job duties

Exercise 1 page 92

server: serves food
mechanic: fixes cars
salesperson: sells clothes
receptionist: answers the phone
custodian: cleans buildings
cashier: counts money

Exercise 2 page 92

1. serves food
2. answers the phone
3. counts money
4. sells clothes
5. cleans buildings
6. fixes cars

Exercise 3 page 92

1. fixes cars
2. sells clothes
3. serves food

Exercise 4 page 93

1. sells clothes
2. cleans buildings
3. counts money
4. serves food
5. answers the phone
6. fixes cars

Lesson C: Does he sell clothes?

Exercise 1 page 94

1. a   4. a
2. a   5. b
3. b   6. a

Exercise 2 page 95

1A. Does, serve
1B. does
2A. Does, count
2B. does
3A. Does, answer
3B. doesn't
4A. Does, clean
4B. does
5A. Does, fix
5B. doesn't
6A. Does, sell
6B. does

Lesson D: Reading

Exercise 1 page 96

1. sells clothes, salesperson
2. fixes cars, mechanic
3. counts money, cashier
4. serves food, waiter
5. answers the phone, receptionist

Exercise 2 page 97

1. truck driver
2. homemaker
3. plumber
4. teacher's aide
5. bus driver
6. painter

Lesson E: Writing

Exercise 1 page 98

1. sells   4. fixes
2. counts   5. cleans
3. serves   6. drives

Exercise 2 page 98

1. clothes   5. cars
2. food   6. bus
3. buildings   7. phone
4. money

Exercise 3 page 98

1. custodian, buildings
2. cashier, money
3. bus driver, bus

Exercise 4 page 99

1. server
2. serves
3. bus driver
4. drives
5. salesperson
6. sell

Exercise 5 page 99

1. Rita
2. Tamar
3. Levon

Lesson F: Another view

Exercise 1 page 100

1. A   3. B   5. B
2. C   4. A   6. A

Exercise 2 page 101

```
m e c h a n i c
        o
        m
        s e r v e r
p l u m b e r
        p a i n t e r
        k
c a s h i e r
    b u s d r i v e r
```

Exercise 3 page 101

1. bus driver, drives a bus
2. cashier, counts money
3. mechanic, fixes cars
4. truck driver, drives a truck

Unit 9: Daily living

Lesson A: Listening

Exercise 1 page 102

1. dishes   4. laundry
2. homework   5. bed
3. lunch   6. dishes

Exercise 2 page 102

1. making lunch
2. doing homework
3. washing the dishes

Exercise 3 page 102

1. washing   4. drying
2. making   5. making
3. doing   6. doing

Exercise 4 page 103

Top to bottom: 6, 3, 2, 5, 1, 4

Exercise 5 page 103

1. drying the dishes
2. doing the laundry
3. doing homework
4. washing the dishes
5. making lunch
6. making the bed

Lesson B: Outside chores

Exercise 1 page 104
1. cutting
2. getting
3. taking
4. walking
5. watering
6. washing

Exercise 2 page 104
1. cutting the grass
2. taking out the trash
3. getting the mail
4. walking the dog
5. watering the grass
6. washing the car

Exercise 3 page 105
1. Watering
2. Cutting
3. Getting
4. Washing
5. Taking
6. Walking

Lesson C: What are they doing?

Exercise 1 page 106
1. drying the dishes
2. making the bed
3. getting the mail
4. taking out the trash
5. washing the car
6. doing the laundry
7. cutting the grass
8. walking the dog

Exercise 2 page 106
1A. are
1B. mail
2A. is
2B. dinner
3A. is
3B. grass
4A. are
4B. dishes
5A. is
5B. dog
6A. is
6B. trash

Exercise 3 page 107
1A. is
1B. Making
2A. are
2B. Making

3A. is
3B. Getting
4A. are
4B. Cutting
5A. is
5B. Washing
6A. is
6B. Taking

Lesson D: Reading

Exercise 1 page 108
1. No
2. Yes
3. No
4. Yes
5. Yes

Exercise 2 page 108
1. washing the car
2. washing the dishes
3. cutting the grass
4. doing homework
5. taking out the trash

Exercise 3 page 109
1. bathroom
2. bedroom
3. living room
4. laundry room
5. kitchen
6. dining room

Exercise 4 page 109
1. kitchen
2. bedroom
3. kitchen
4. laundry room
5. kitchen

Lesson E: Writing

Exercise 1 page 110
1. drying
2. washing
3. making
4. doing
5. making
6. doing

Exercise 2 page 110
1. doing homework
2. making the bed

3. drying the dishes
4. washing the dishes
5. doing the laundry
6. making lunch

Exercise 3 page 111
Justin: doing the laundry
Melissa: washing the dishes
Henry: doing homework
Penny: making lunch
Bill: making the bed
Erica: drying the dishes

Lesson F: Another view

Exercise 1 page 112
1. B
2. A
3. C
4. A
5. C

Exercise 2 page 112
1. is washing
2. is making
3. is taking
4. is cutting
5. is doing

Exercise 3 page 113
1. bathroom
2. bedroom
3. kitchen
4. dining room
5. living room
6. laundry room

Exercise 4 page 113
1. kitchen
2. laundry room
3. kitchen
4. bedroom
5. kitchen

Exercise 5 page 113
Chores inside the house: drying the dishes, making lunch, making the bed, washing the dishes

Chores outside the house: cutting the grass, walking the dog, washing the car, watering the grass

Unit 10: Free time

Lesson A: Listening

Exercise 1 page 114
1. fish
2. swim
3. dance
4. exercise
5. play cards
6. play basketball

Exercise 2 page 114

```
b i c y t a b l s h
p d a n c e y z f i
e x e r p l a y m b
e x e r c i s e d o
c a r d s m o n w t
e y f i s w i m y a
d a v n g e l u s w
n c f i s h i m b a
b a s k e t b a l l
d s z o n f r e x p
```

Exercise 3 page 115
Top to bottom: 2, 4, 5, 1, 3
1. swim
2. play basketball
3. play cards
4. fish
5. exercise

Lesson B: Around the house

Exercise 1 page 116
1. read magazines
2. play the guitar
3. listen to music
4. watch TV
5. work in the garden

Exercise 2 page 116
1. music
2. TV
3. the guitar
4. in the garden
5. magazines

Exercise 3 page 117
1. Cook
2. Listen to music
3. Read magazines
4. Play the guitar
5. Work in the garden
6. Watch TV

Lesson C: I like to watch TV.

Exercise 1 page 118
1. likes
2. likes
3. like
4. likes
5. like
6. like
7. likes
8. like

Exercise 2 page 119
1. likes, exercise
2. likes, cook
3. likes, swim
4. likes, fish
5. like, dance
6. like, play cards

Lesson D: Reading

Exercise 1 page 120
1. Yes
2. No
3. No
4. No
5. Yes
6. Yes

Exercise 2 page 121
1. volunteer
2. go to the movies
3. exercise
4. travel
5. shop

Lesson E: Writing

Exercise 1 page 122
1. swim
2. fish
3. cook
4. shop
5. dance
6. volunteer

Exercise 2 page 122
1. work in the garden
2. swim
3. volunteer
4. fish
5. play cards

Exercise 3 page 123
1. play
2. watch
3. read
4. go
5. visit
6. exercise
7. listen to

Exercise 4 page 123
Sunday: go to the movies
Monday: exercise
Tuesday: listen to music
Wednesday: read magazines
Thursday: watch TV
Friday: visit friends
Saturday: play basketball

Lesson F: Another view

Exercise 1 page 124
1. A
2. C
3. B
4. A
5. B
6. A

Exercise 2 page 125
1. play cards
2. visit friends
3. play the guitar
4. read magazines
5. play basketball
6. listen to music

Exercise 3 page 125
Costs money: travel, go to the movies, shop
No money: run, visit friends, volunteer

Exercise 4 page 125
Exercise: dance, play basketball, play soccer, run, swim
No exercise: go online, listen to music, play cards, read magazines, watch TV

ACKNOWLEDGEMENTS

The authors and publishers acknowledge the following sources of copyright material and are grateful for the permissions granted. While every effort has been made, it has not always been possible to identify the sources of all the material used, or to trace all copyright holders. If any omissions are brought to our notice, we will be happy to include the appropriate acknowledgements on reprinting and in the next update to the digital edition, as applicable.

Key: T = Top, TL = Top Left, TC = Top Center, TR = Top Right, BL = Below Left, BC = Below Center, BR = Below Right, C = Center, L = Left, R = Right, CR = Center Right, CL = Center Left, Ex = Exercise.

Photos

All images are sourced from Getty Images.

p. 5 (Ex 6.6): Cover image from ventures SB 3rd edition; p. 6: Nancy Brown/Photographer's Choice; p. 10 (L): wickedpix/iStock/Getty Images Plus; p. 10 (R): Purestock; p. 11: PhotoAlto/Eric Audras/PhotoAlto Agency RF Collections; p. 14: Plan Shoot/Multi-bits/The Image Bank; p. 15: Plush Studios/Bill Reitzel/Blend Images; p. 18 (Ex 1.1): Jon Boyes/Photographer's Choice RF; p.18 (Ex 1.2): OverShoot/iStock/Getty Images Plus; p.18 (Ex 1.3): kwanchaichaiudom/iStock/Getty Images Plus; p. 18 (Ex 1.4): Cover image from ventures SB 3rd edition; p. 18 (Ex 1.5): Tetra Images; p. 30 (TL): Terry Vine/Blend Images; p. 30 (TR): Gilbert Rondilla Photography/Moment; p. 30 (CL): diego_cervo/iStock/Getty Images Plus; p. 30 (CR): m-imagephotography/iStock/Getty Images Plus; p. 30 (BL): Jupiterimages/Polka Dot/Getty Images Plus; p. 30 (BR): GlobalStock/iStock / Getty Images Plus; p. 32: Mike Kemp/Blend Images; p. 41: Indeed; p. 42 (TL): Jose Luis Pelaez Inc/Blend Images; p. 42 (TR): Hero Images; p. 42 (CL): Thomas Northcut/DigitalVision; p. 42 (CR): Sean Russell; p. 42 (BL): LWA/Dann Tardif/Blend Images; p. 42 (BR): ERproductions Ltd/Blend Images; p. 54 (Ex 1.1): andresr/E+; p. 54 (Ex 1.2): WALTER ZERLA/Cultura; p. 54 (Ex 1.3): Westend61; p. 54 (Ex 1.4): Dan Dalton/Caiaimage; p. 54 (Ex 1.5): Peter Cade/The Image Bank; p. 65: haoliang/E+;p. 72: Cover image from ventures SB 3rd edition; p. 79 (Ex 1.1): thirty_three/iStock/Getty Images Plus; p. 79 (Ex 1.2): GaryAlvis/E+; p. 79 (Ex 1.3): domin_domin/iStock/Getty Images Plus; p. 79 (Ex 1.4): Lalouetto/iStock/Getty Images Plus; p. 79 (Ex 1.5): ARSELA/E+; p. 79 (Ex 1.6): Issaurinko/iStock/Getty Images Plus; p. 93 (TL): Bambu Productions/The Image Bank; p. 93 (TR), p. 94 (BL): AndreyPopov/iStock/Getty Images Plus; p. 93 (CL): Jose Luis Pelaez Inc/Blend Images; p. 93 (CR): Dan Dalton/Caiaimage; p. 93 (BL): PhotoAlto/Frederic Cirou/PhotoAlto Agency RF Collections; p. 93 (BR): Reza Estakhrian/Iconica; p. 94 (TL): Jetta Productions/Blend Images; p. 94 (TR): Jose Luis Pelaez Inc./Blend Images; p. 94 (CL): Cultura RM Exclusive/yellowdog/Cultura Exclusive; p. 94 (CR): Hero Images; p. 94 (BR): kali9/E+; p. 99 (T): Wavebreakmedia Ltd/Wavebreak Media/Getty Images Plus; p. 99 (C): kali9/E+; p. 99 (B): filadendron/E+; p. 102 (L): Jupiterimages/Stockbyte; p. 102 (C): Morsa Images/DigitalVision; p. 102 (R): Maskot; p. 105 (TL): Martyn Rose/The Image Bank; p. 105 (TR): Westend61; p. 105 (CL): M_a_y_a/E+; p. 105 (CR): Image Source/DigitalVision; p. 105 (BL): Ben-Schonewille/iStock/Getty Images Plus; p. 105 (BR): Bruce Laurance/The Image Bank; p. 108: Fuse; p. 118: Westend61; p. 119 (TL): Caiaimage/Robert Daly; p. 119 (TR): Betsie Van der Meer/Iconica; p. 119 (CL): Peter Cade/The Image Bank; p. 119 (CR): cjp/E+; p. 119 (BL): Mike Harrington/The Image Bank; p. 119 (BR): Jupiterimages/Photolibrary; p. 120 (L): Vladimir Godnik; p. 120 (C): Sam Edwards/Caiaimage; p. 120 (R): Johnny Greig/E+.

Illustrations

p. 3, p. 22, p. 50, p. 59, p. 63, p. 72, p. 73 and p. 111: Kevin Brown; p. 5 (Ex 6.1–6.5, 6.7 and 6.8) and p. 58: Phil Williams; p. 5 (Ex 6.6), p. 8, p. 9, p. 19, p. 20, p. 23, p. 31, p. 37, p. 43, p. 47 (Ex 4.1–4.6), p. 55, p. 60, p. 62, p. 66, p. 67, p.78 (Ex 2), p. 88, p. 103 and p. 112: QBS Learning; p. 21, p. 29 (Ex 2.1–2.8), p. 36, p. 48, p. 49, p. 98, p. 107 and p. 115: John Batten; p. 26, p. 44, p. 53, p. 69, p. 80, p. 91, p. 95 and p. 117: Frank Montagna; p. 27 and p. 92 (Ex 3.1, 3.2): William Waitzman; p. 33, p. 38, p. 45 and p. 97: Kim Johnson; p. 34, p. 47 (Ex 3.1–3.5), p.78 (Ex 1.1–1.6), p. 85 and p. 116: Paul Hampson; p. 35, p. 46, p. 61, p. 104 and p. 121: Scott Mooney; p. 39, p. 57,p. 81, p. 86 and p. 109: Ben Hasler; p. 83 and p. 92 (Ex 3.3): Bill Waitzman.

Front Cover Photography by Jetta Productions/Blend Images.

The audio producer is CityVox.